UNLOCKED

UNLOCKED

HOW EMPOWERED WOMEN
EMPOWER WOMEN

JANE FINETTE

NEW DEGREE PRESS

UNLOCKED

How Empowered Women Empower Women

ISBN   978-1-63676-742-0 *Paperback*

           978-1-63730-481-5 *Kindle Ebook*

           978-1-63730-482-2 *Ebook*

*For the strong women who raise us, for the sisters
who hold us, and for all daughters rising.*

CONTENTS

———

Feminism is not a scheme to deprive men, but a campaign to liberate us all.

—REBECCA SOLNIT

INTRODUCTION

HOW IT ALL BEGAN

It all began for me in 1989 in the UK. I was fifteen years old, and I took my first female empowerment action. I lobbied and won the right for girls at my school to wear trousers as part of their school uniform. Yes, you got that right. It was and still is a thing for kids to wear uniforms from age eleven to sixteen in the UK. Even in the middle of winter (when we used to have real winters in the UK pre-climate-crisis), girls were forbidden to have their legs covered. This was not a conservative or religious school, or a cult; it was just an ordinary, secondary modern school like most high schools across the UK. I walked many a winter day to school in a foot of snow with raw cold-burned knees and icy cold other places, as skirts were the only option. What I once considered normal, now seems to me to be straight out of the dystopian TV show *The Handmaid's Tale*, which was equally ridiculous and unjust. It propelled this quiet small-town girl to become a bold female activist.

One particularly frigid winter, we were huddled outside on the playground shivering. I became enraged with anger at our unnecessary suffering. I confidently rallied a group of female school friends to make a challenge. We got ourselves in front of the school's board of governors, and I made an impassioned plea on behalf of all girls that it was a terrible idea to make us wear skirts to school all year round. Not only because of the unforgiving British winters, but also because it was unbearably cold inside the bleak 1980s classrooms. Inside and outside, we shivered for five straight months. I argued that it wasn't conducive to effective concentration and learning. At the time, I thought it was a long shot, but to their credit, they listened and agreed. We won.

It was a revelation to me that things could be different and change could happen. Walls came crashing down, and it hadn't been all that hard, but it took courage and a desire to break the status quo. A small action with a first bold step. My classmates celebrated in school hallways, and I remember taking deep pride and comfort in seeing my fellow sisters showing off their new slacks at school any time of the year! I was fired up.

EXPECTATIONS VERSUS REALITY

My early feminist activism was short-lived. Life carried on and my struggles as a young woman trying and failing to make it in the world while my male friends succeeded became normalized. Discrimination, which was glaringly obvious in my youth, became universal in my early career, but I didn't recognize the pervasive inequality for decades.

On the surface, women in the UK looked like they could do and be anything they wanted. We had a woman as our Queen, and I'd grown up with Margaret Thatcher as prime minister, but they were rarities, which did not reflect the full story.

Twenty-five years ago, off-color jokes about women and race were tolerated, even on prime-time UK TV. I distinctly recall my dad laughing out loud to *The Benny Hill Show* every Saturday night, and the *Carry On* films every holiday—with my mum and grandma laughing along too. We would crowd around the TV each weekend, and watch Benny Hill surrounded by bikini-clad babes and telling jokes like, "Girls are like pianos. When they're not upright, they're grand," and, "I'm not against half-naked girls—not as often as I'd like to be." We would laugh and laugh. It's easy to believe this socially accepted sexist behavior wasn't directly connected to commonplace unwanted sexual advances, the likes of which I was years later often subjected to in the workplace.

When I reexamine my early life, I see a woman who was completely immersed in experiencing as many things as possible. While I often experienced the pang of bias and discrimination, I did not expect to create change. It was no longer as easy as my quick, youthful victory had been. So, the light I had focused and shone as a wronged teenager on the plight of women and girls went dark. It would take thirty more years for me to pick up the mantle and get my torch relit.

It was true, women in the Western world had gained more freedoms since the 1960s, and that was also so in the UK. In the liberating 1960s, The British Library chronicled that UK women gained access to the contraceptive pill, abortion was legalized, and— via the Married Women's Property Act— women were finally allowed to be the legal owners of money they earned. After the first recorded strike by women over equal pay in 1968 at the Ford factory in Dagenham, the UK brought in equal pay legislation. However, until this present day, there remains a big difference between the liberties we have been awarded in principle and what we can expect in practice. Today, women in the UK continue to endure gender-based violence, as Alexandra Topping in The Guardian reported in March 2021, they are still fighting for the right to feel safe on the UK's streets even from the police who are meant to protect them, and protesting the right to expect equal treatment in the workplace.

In fact, 110 years after the suffragette movement when women finally won the right to vote, women in the West are still fighting for equal rights, equal opportunity, ownership of our bodies, and so much more. That's all without examining the appalling lack of human rights of women in the developing world. Leticia Pfeffer from Global Citizen reported back in 2014, 70 percent of the world's poorest one billion people are women. Alarmingly, the World Economic Forum stated in 2021, if the same rate of progress continues, it will take another 257 years to close the global gender equity gap.

IT'S GOING TO TAKE ALL OF US

This is where I found myself in the middle of the worldwide COVID-19 pandemic, reading news article after article of women's rights going backward not forward. I was despondent hearing that women were dropping out of the workforce by the millions, shocked by reports of intensified sexual violence, and heartbroken at the erosion of girls' rights to go to school. I faced the fact that women had lost a generation of progress in the past twelve months alone, and it was going to take decades to claw back already slim gains.

I wrote this book because we cannot wait 257 years for women to be equal. To make significant and lasting change happen, we need new legislation, people, businesses, and governments to be held accountable. We need to work together to make gender and racial bias a thing of the past. Each and every one of us can actively take progress into our own hands. Women helping women, en masse, on every level, is a massive groundswell of change that we can all be part of, and by the hundreds of thousands cannot be ignored. When all women take progress into their own hands, it's my belief we can reach global gender equity within this generation.

After two decades of building global consumer brands such as eBay and Mozilla, and founding several companies of my own, my work supporting women was reignited in 2014 when I founded the global nonprofit, The Coaching Fellowship. We give young women leaders in social change critical access to leadership development. I like to say, we help the helpers, who range from women rehabilitating child-soldiers in Sierra Leone, to climate activists in Boston, to women protecting the rights of indigenous people throughout Latin America. Over the past seven years, my team and I have helped over 1,100 women nonprofit leaders, social entrepreneurs, and female activists from seventy plus countries. I witnessed firsthand the challenges they have experienced and the great impact they have created.

I've learned a great deal by empowering women leaders from all over the world at different stages of growth, working in different fields with different needs. The core of what stands out for me every single time is that every woman already had all she needed to succeed within her. What she really needed was a deep well of other women around her to believe in her potential, to help her help herself, to hold her feet to the fire to take action, and then continuously call her forward. That is something we all have the power to do for every woman in our lives, and it can bring untold progress, opportunity, and change.

Research after study after report shows that when women are empowered, the world gets better. If more women sit at the negotiating table, there is less war and more sustaining peace. When women are given access to the resources they need for agricultural production, food security increases, says USAID. Leticia Pfeffer from Global Citizen, again in 2014, claimed giving women farmers more rights would reduce the number of hungry people in the world by 150 million. Also, empowered women lead to less deaths from childbirth and lower infant mortality rates. They reduce illiteracy, and when women and girls reach gender equity, USAID reports they could increase global GDP by $12 trillion by 2025. There's even a notion from the Rainforest Alliance that more empowered women will solve the climate crisis.

Women and girls create virtuous circles and create a ripple effect around them. When women are empowered, they pour their energy, skills, time, and money back into their communities. In the developing world, Global Citizen reports women reinvest up to 90 percent of their incomes back into their families, compared to 30–40 percent by men. It seems to me there is no silver bullet for tackling the global grand challenges of today, but advancing women and girls comes pretty darn close. Therefore, we all must strive to bring forward more empowered women.

WILL YOU JOIN ME?

If, like me, you are concerned by gender equity going backward, not forward, and if you want to do something about it but don't know how or where to start, I hope this book can provide some answers. First, through sharing real-world impactful stories, I hope to restore your faith that despite the news stories and dire statistics, positive change is actually happening for women and girls. In Part I, you will meet brilliant women such as Holly Gordon, an ABC News producer who was forced to quit her dream job when balancing motherhood and her career became impossible. Ever resilient, she founded the global movement *Girl Rising* in 2013, working to ensure girls around the world are educated and empowered. And, women like Tracy Chou, the accidental activist and now entrepreneur who kick-started the diversity debate in Silicon Valley. I'm excited for you to hear about their journeys and achievements.

Second, in Part II, I will share ten easy, practical, and repeatable keys to help another woman succeed. These are empowering actions you can start taking today, which I hope will prove that you can make a difference. I'll describe how to take a stand, actually talk about money, and many more simple and impactful steps. If you are concerned you alone cannot affect change, I hope to show you how you can be part of the groundswell of change led by women for women. Female empowerment doesn't need any special training. It only requires us to act, do it with conviction, and do it often. This is the root and the heart behind achieving gender equality.

With an endless list of issues facing all women today, I do not profess to have all the answers. I have impressions, ideas, and actions taken from my own experiences, and from some of today's most brilliant women leaders supporting women forward. It's my honor to share a collection of their stories, some who I have had the pleasure of knowing and working with for decades. Some are new friends introduced to me by women wanting to help me write this book. They are women who have shaped me personally, women who are shaping society at large today, and a path for women and girls to succeed in their wake.

In my interviews, I have been enraged with injustice and moved to tears by stories of suffering and loss. I've been humbled by the hard work and risk-taking for progress and inspired beyond measure by such meaningful work done. In sum, I hold an overwhelming sense of joy and hope that change is happening like never before. May you find inspiration in the stories I share and be energized to take many small and empowering actions that will make a difference to another woman's life.

Writing this book in the wake of the COVID-19 pandemic, racial injustice, economic inequalities, and the climate crisis laid bare, it's hardly surprising that women see women as the answer and want us to be part of the solution, fast. It has become clear that patriarchal systems do not benefit the whole of society. The need for women to be in positions of leadership at levels equal to men has never been more urgent. Why? Because when we are, the world is fairer, more sustainable and equitable for everyone.

Women create virtuous circles and there has been a great outpouring of women wanting to help me with this book. They helped me see it could be in service of a new wave of collective and personal action for us.

When each of us as women see ourselves as activists, a groundswell of changes becomes not just possible, but inevitable. Whether you are a leader in business, in the social impact space, in the nonprofit realm, or are just starting out, you can make a difference. Together, our actions, by the hundreds of thousands, will indeed create enough progress in this generation to reach global gender equity.

My sincerest wish for this book is that it activates every woman, everywhere, to take progress into her own hands. May every woman hear the call to lift up all sisters on the rising tide, and help them chart a path forward for the sake of all girls.

We rise by lifting others.

PART I

STORIES TO INSPIRE

CHAPTER 1

WHERE IT ALL BEGINS

Feminism isn't about making women stronger.
Women are already strong, it's about changing
the way the world perceives that strength.

—G.D. ANDERSON

Let's start with a question. As a woman, who was the first most-empowered woman who empowered you? For some of us, it is our mom, for others, maybe it was another female in the family such as a grandmother, sister, or aunt who nurtured and inspired us as girls. Maybe some found their biggest nurturer and fierce defender as teenagers in their schools, communities, or places of worship. Some of us found those powerful women later in their twenties, thirties, and beyond, often at our place of work.

These generous, empowered women taught us, led by example, and motivated us to reach beyond what we thought was possible for ourselves. I have witnessed and experienced the positive impact of women empowering other women, and I've made it my life's purpose to encourage this phenomenon to spread and become commonplace. Today, many women are going it alone, without the wind at their backs that a female mentor, colleague, or friend can create. I want to change that. In my ideal world, every woman has the support, encouragement, and nurturing they need to reach their full potential.

When I started writing this book, I first wanted to examine the key women who had deeply influenced me and made me who I am. And yes, my mum not only created every fiber of my being, she has been, and still is, the single most empowering woman in my life.

We all know what it feels like to be held and uplifted, no matter our age, by someone who wants us to live our best life. Whether that was our mother, or another inspirational woman, it's good to take a moment and place ourselves in the shoes of our most significant female advocates. How wonderful to feel all the energy, experiences, and desires they had to help us. The joy of giving to another woman or girl can be a sacred act.

Less than a handful of women deeply empowered me throughout my life. I sought to examine their most significant contributions and assess if there were any connected threads. One thing stood out immediately as I considered the major female influences on me over the past four and a half decades. It was not their power and influence, their expertise and experience, or their wealth and privilege, although a handful definitely had some or all of these. The underlying and unifying characteristic was their belief in me and my potential in this world.

EXPERTS IN HOLDING UP A MIRROR

Every single woman who helped me on my path saw something in me that I couldn't see for myself. They have all been experts in holding up a mirror, calling me forward toward my greatness, and helping me make it happen by myself. Their championing of me was constant, their encouragement was unwavering, and their belief I would do great things was expressed whenever possible.

What was fascinating about this discovery was that I had thought there would be numerous momentous occasions to point to, such as a reckoning where they helped me face the music, a point where several doors opened, a killer piece of advice given, a skill taught, or a grand intervention. But actually, those who had the greatest influence did so in what appears at first as tiny, small, quiet ways, which led me to take big steps on my own from founding companies to moving countries. The cumulative effect of these few women and their daily support over the years created everything from a soft landing, to a sharp focus, and a deep well of encouragement, which buoyed me forward. Sometimes they wanted my success and fulfillment more than I wanted it for myself. It made all the difference in the actions I took.

It's important to note, the very act of empowerment can be as subtle as a kind word, a look that says, "you've got this," or an example that shows what's possible. My women champions have been my safety net. They cheered me on when I first raised the idea of changing careers and urged me not to give up when I thought I was going to lose my organization to the pandemic. As women, we can give advice and invest our money and our time to advance one another, but let's not forget how much acts of kindness can move mountains. Professional women acting like a loving sister and caring as they would for their own family, that's a powerful act of taking progress into our own hands.

When we think about advancing women, it is typically in big ways that we think we are incapable of affecting. However, there are also a myriad of small actions that are completely within our reach, which are entirely possible if we do them every day for any woman we meet.

As the years passed by, a multitude of incredible women have come in and out of my life. Women like Tracy DeMiroz who rescued me emotionally, if not physically, from my death spiral at Mozilla when I had moved halfway around the world for a job, to my surprise on arrival which no longer existed. To Jessilyn Davis, profoundly wise for her age, who worked for me for years and taught me how to laugh every single day. To Sharon Vosmek who took a chance on me and gave me an opportunity to become an entrepreneur in residence to explore what I might bring into the world next. These women have been my work colleagues, women in my network, old work friends, and one was a phenomenal executive coach. Most recently, they have been the board of directors at my organization, The Coaching Fellowship. They have helped me grow into a leader who can serve more women. They all helped me reach the next stage of my growth with their openness to support me and by acting from a place of love.

In the past decade, two things changed noticeably for me, and that's when my career and life began thriving. First, I asked women for help, which was something I was uncomfortable doing for a long time as a female leader. It was extraordinary to me that when I asked, women gladly supported me and would then go out of their way to help make connections, share ideas, and generously point out my mistakes. Second, I began purposely and intentionally empowering other women. I would lend a hand, call out their achievements, and show support if they failed.

For example, for years, I'd play a game to dish out as many compliments as I could every day to different women when I noticed something that moved me. I made a point to acknowledge skills and a job well done, above any physical attribute like her clothes or her hair. It was satisfying to see a wide smile break across her face, and a look that said, "Thank you for seeing me." It's hard to underestimate how much confidence and self-esteem are increased for women when the great work they do is finally acknowledged. A 2018 report by Claire Shipman, Katty Kay, and JillEllyn Riley in *The Atlantic*, showed that girls' self-worth peaks at age twelve and quickly declines by 30 percent, and this dramatic lack of feeling self-assured can last through adulthood. Small acts can help support a woman feel valued and, thus, increase self-esteem.

THE ROAD TO PROGRESS IS NOT LINEAR

We do not need to be the CEO of a Fortune 500 company, have millions of dollars to spend, or be a legislator putting forward new laws and rights to be an empowered woman who supports another. Yes, it matters, we need more women in those positions of influence. But it is a misconception that the vast majority of us cannot help, that our acts do not count, and that it will not make a difference when we reach out to help.

"Never doubt that a small group of thoughtful, committed citizens can change the world: indeed, it's the only thing that ever has."

—MARGARET MEAD

As I've explained using the example of our moms, and mom-like figures, we know the power of someone who helps us make our own choices and chart our own path. We know the sisterhood of girlfriends who we can call when we need kind words, to simply vent, and to get pointed again in the right direction. These simple acts are no different for our female colleagues at work and for women in our wider network. They too need our support and encouragement. We can be the difference that helps them push through and gives them the courage to keep going. Whether we bravely actually talk about money, tell her she is ready, give her confidence, or simply be the example, we each can take progress into our own hands by empowering another woman.

I am not naive, and neither are you. The challenges for women are deep-rooted and vast, and they will require continued action throughout the world on every level. We have already been working tirelessly for almost two hundred years. A lot of progress has been made, but we still have a very long way to go. The road to progress has not been linear and never will be; there have been twists and turns, lost ways found again, and still much success. The world for women looks very different from how it did just fifty years ago. The important part of a journey is to keep moving forward and, in today's world, use what we have in abundance to create change.

A WHIRLWIND HISTORY OF FEMALE EMPOWERMENT

The history of female empowerment in the Western world began with the suffragette movements in the late nineteenth and early twentieth century to win the right to vote for women. Elizabeth Smiltneek explains in her Learning to Give resource that it was rooted in the abolition of slavery. In the United States, it became a seventy-two-year-long battle. The movement promoted civic action among newly enfranchised women whose ripple effect touched following generations who fought for education rights, civil rights, and healthcare reforms. Their actions led to the first wave of feminism, which spread throughout the world.

The second wave came in the 1960s when the invention of the birth control pill coincided with a period of sexual liberation, and women gained control over their bodies, and their future. Prior to the pill being widely available, a large number of women did not even complete their education. But with legal access to the pill, Planned Parenthood described women's "college enrollment was 20 percent higher" and the dropout rate between 1969 and 1980 was "35 percent lower than women without access to the pill." As women completed their education, they ultimately gained professional careers, and as the Planned Parenthood paper continued, "the pill was also a major driver in women pursuing medicine, dentistry, and law."

The third wave of feminism rose on the backdrop of Anita Hill's testimony in front of an all-male, all-white US Senate Judiciary Committee, recounting to the world in 1991 the sexual harassment she experienced by Supreme Court Justice nominee Clarence Thomas. All this, while The Spice Girls were topping the charts with their girl power motivated songs and taking the world by storm. In 1995, at the Fourth World Conference on Women in Beijing, with thirty thousand activists in attendance, Hillary Clinton (then first lady), said publicly "women's rights are human rights"—a slogan she took from the group Gabriela (a coalition of Filipino women).

The event was a crucible moment when the definition of feminism expanded to include all races beyond only white women, and it kicked off the decentralization of female activism using the internet. It taught conference goers how to get online and, as a result, women's online activities soared throughout the world. According to Lisa Levenstein, author of the 2020 book, *They Didn't See Us Coming,* "By the end of the 1990s, anyone looking for feminism no longer needed to attend a march or a conference... all they needed was a modem, a computer, and a phone line." The nineties changed the conversation for women's empowerment both in terms of where and what conversations were being had.

In recent years, feminism has reached a level of cultural significance it hasn't seen in years. It began in 2006 with the #MeToo social movement that was started by Tarana Burke against sexual abuse and sexual harassment toward women. The sheer number of supporters and the visibility they created led to high-profile sex offenders like film director Harvey Weinstein being convicted of rape and sentenced to prison for twenty-three years in 2020. A few years later, the Women's March received mass support by spearheading the resistance against newly elected Donald Trump. Only a few days after the march in January 2017, Matt Broomfield, at *The Independent,* reported it was the largest single-day protest in US history. Since then, there are annual women's marches that follow in the footsteps of the early emancipated advocates for a range of civil and human rights issues.

Feminism and women's empowerment are now firmly part of the cultural discourse where actresses, musicians, and sports stars speak up and often for our rights. From Emma Watson, the outspoken female activist and UN Women Goodwill ambassador who launched the UN Women campaign HeForShe in 2014, which urged men to advocate for gender equality, to Patricia Arquette, who made headlines in 2015 for her Oscars speech on wage equality. Hollywood's gender pay gap is one of the most significant. Jamie Doward, at The Guardian, reported in 2019 that male stars earn one million dollars more per film than women. Sports closely follow. In March 2019, Megan Rapinoe, American professional soccer player and captain of the US national team, along with twenty-seven of her US Women's soccer teammates, filed a lawsuit against the United States Soccer Federation accusing it of gender discrimination.

These movements to advance women, especially those in recent history, have gone far to change laws, rights, politics, and attitudes toward women's human rights, our legal rights, and reproductive rights. It is no surprise, however, that there is still a very long way to go. Due to the impact of the COVID-19 pandemic, women and girls have lost more than a generation of progress in 2020 alone. But it is still important to reflect and see how far we have come. When I think back on my four decades on this earth, I've seen gay marriage legalized in many countries, and the vast majority of the stigma surrounding LGBTQ+ disappear. I've seen gender stereotyping banned from adverts. There have been all-women space walks, a black woman won an Oscar for Best Actress, and just this year (2021), we saw the youngest self-made female billionaire at thirty-one, and the first woman to be elected vice president in US history, who also happens to be a Black and South Asian American.

We have much to celebrate, and while there are still big jobs to do for women's equality worldwide, the work is now to get the flywheel of change turning faster. The virtuous circles we, as women, create will inspire more action and create the change we are seeking.

Now let's meet some incredible women who, on their many varied journeys, are creating lasting change for women and girls. Whether that's been through creating access to skills, opportunities, capital, voice, networks, or leverage. I hope you will see these women are also just like you and me. They face personal challenges, they're trying to do it all, make it all, and be it all. They all began with a small bold step, which over time became an earth-shattering moment. I chose to share a collection of their stories to inspire and encourage you. Reading stories of courage, success, and fortitude will help you see change is possible. Learning how to take small, daily, empowering actions will make it a reality.

We are the ones we have been waiting for. Let's dive in.

CHAPTER 2

GOING FAR TOGETHER

———

Alone, we can do so little;
together, we can do so much.

—HELEN KELLER

Why is it when women hear the word "networking" we feel a deep resistance, the likes of doing our taxes or cleaning the inside of the car? This was my personal experience. I was never good at small talk, I hated name badges, and the scant exchanges. When speed networking became a thing, I simply checked out completely. Networking seems like the scourge of the earth for most of us, and yet we are known as relationship experts. We love helping people and connecting, but mention the word networking, and we will run for the hills.

Networking is wrapped up in so much. We get stuck in how it seems inauthentic, transactional, like we're selfish, and using someone for personal gain. A research paper first published in 2014 by Tiziana Casciaro, Francesca Gino, and Maryam

Kouchaki shows networking can make us feel dirty, and therefore a bad person. A focus on building a network is not a priority for women for many reasons. According to a December 2017 research paper written by Julio Mancuso Tradenta, Ananta Neelim, and Joe Vecci entitled "Gender Differences in Self-Promotion, "it can start with our beliefs that we have little to offer or show up as gendered modesty and we won't put ourselves out there because self-promotion appears brazen." It's easy to see if we don't enjoy it, think we're bad, and have nothing to offer—then we are less likely to make time for it in our already busy schedules. The bottom line is women aren't networking enough, and we are missing out.

NETWORKING BY THE NUMBERS

Evidence confirms the power of networks is key to professional advancement. A study by the Adler Group and LinkedIn showed 85 percent of jobs are filled through networking. That number was so surprising to me until I stopped to consider the last time I formally searched and was interviewed for a job, which was at the age of twenty-five, so I would have to agree. Networks beget networks, and the more people you know, the more opportunities are possible. When I also think about the people I've hired and the volunteers who work with me at The Coaching Fellowship, the vast majority were known from network introductions. The good news is that things are changing, and a new way of networking is happening.

In a 2020 article about networking being a critical skill, Jeffrey Pfeffer, professor of organizational behavior at Stanford University, explains how strong networks and your networking skills relate to your current salary and the growth of your salary over time. They affect your chances of receiving top performance reviews, how likely you are to be promoted, and how likely you might be retained by a company. It's hard to underestimate the importance of the people you know and the people who know you.

So, women might not enjoy networking and are not overly focused on seeking it out, but that can't be the only reason it's hard for us to build, retain, and utilize a network. I spoke with Herminia Ibarra, professor of organizational behavior at London Business School, to find out what else could go on. Back in the eighties, she was one of the first to observe how women's networks differed from men's in the workplace and how that influenced their career success.

Her PhD research focused on informal networks inside organizations and how they affected innovation. "To my great surprise it turned out the new ideas which were implemented came through people who were really centrally placed in these networks." Most were male leaders. Herminia explains they had both a strong network outside the company with professional organizations where idea generation and knowledge got sparked. They also had a strong foot inside their companies, which ensured enough clout that their ideas were first heard and then acted upon. Connections had looked different for women.

Herminia got curious and tried to get underneath what was causing women's lack of access to network, and thus what was holding them back in their career. The big difference had to do with "homophily," a principle that attracts and binds people together similar to themselves. Herminia shared that men's key circles will often overlap between personal and professional, like on the golf course or at professional members group gatherings. This makes it hard for women to connect, therefore both in the workplace or in any other social setting.

She noted women have to work much harder to build connections because we don't have an immediate "click" or have many things in common. She recounts a personal story of her being one of the few senior women faculty members at a previous role. Her peer male colleagues would play football together each week and go to the sauna afterward. She was always the last to know about informal gossip.

Herminia continued, "Gender is an important aspect of similarity. The big difference was that men had access to people in power who were like them." In a 2017 blog post she wrote for the Eve Program, she explains, "women had networks, but their connections were at the lowest levels." They tended to be more personal in nature, were not strategic connections and could not help the person advance their career. These deeply personal relationships at work were not easily portable to a new job. Herminia explains, "men had networks which they could take with them, women had to start from square one."

In early 2021, Alyssa Newcomb for NBC News reported only forty-one women lead Fortune 500 companies, and only three of them are women of color. With a dearth of women in leadership positions, it is time to redesign the power structure and how we network to help each other succeed. Thankfully, there are now hosts of organizations creating space for high-powered networks for women.

WOMEN WANT A DIFFERENT KIND OF NETWORK

Lindsay Kaplan had been VP of Communications and Brand at Casper, the disruptive direct-to-consumer mattress company, when she first met Carolyn Childers. She would become her cofounder at Chief.com, a private network they created to support high-level professional women to connect, get access to resources, and drive more women into positions of power. We were talking on the phone. Lindsay is a night owl and it's early, so no Zoom video. She paints a picture of her morning—getting her toddler up, feeding her new baby—there's little time for herself to be "Zoom ready." She has spoken publicly and honestly about being a "stay-at-home-Mum." In her interview with Ellen Sherberg at BizJournal in 2020—in the middle of the COVID-19 pandemic—she expressed the challenges it created balancing childcare and running a multimillion-dollar company.

Her willingness to share her personal stories as a mom and business leader are part of the reason I am drawn to Lindsay. She epitomizes a strong and authentic female leader of our generation who celebrates motherhood and is completely transparent about her experiences as a female leader. Lindsay is helping her sisters rise in all ways and building a wildly successful business.

Before she cofounded Chief, Lindsay looked like a powerhouse on the outside. She had a team of twenty people and ran marketing for the latest new consumer brands. Lindsey shared with me that although she was satisfied and happy, she was also struggling. She confided there was a hefty "mix of imposter syndrome and paranoia around my decisions." She had a burning desire to continue her career path and support other women she was leading to come up through the ranks, but she herself had no one to turn to and mentor her forward. It was true what they said, it was more than lonely at the top.

Then she met Carolyn. They had discussed their professional experiences and lack of opportunity to advance their careers and feel supported while doing so. They wanted to create a space where executive women could connect, grow, and help each other thrive. Be that leading to new business opportunities, new jobs, board positions, investment, and more. She shared a funny story about when they initially pitched their company to raise investment capital, the investors challenged them to bring in one hundred of their own network to the platform. That did not seem like too much of an ask, however, as Lindsey lamented, "We kind of laughed because between us, we didn't even have a hundred women in our network. That was the exact problem we were trying to solve!" Lindsay shared that with all that being said, what most surprised them was just how many people signed up on day one as a response to their cold email invitations. It demonstrated the desire and need for a network dedicated exclusively to women in professional leadership positions. Their first paying client was a senior woman in the C-Suite of a Fortune 50 company.

Women were interested in networking, and they were willing to pay. They wanted to do it in a way that worked for them. An explicitly female led space, Chief's success lay in bringing women together from different roles across different industries and functions to connect and support one another.

It's clear women and their networks are now big business. To date, Chief is only three years old, and according to Jordan Crook, reporting for *TechCrunch,* in May 2020, it has raised forty million dollars in investment funding and has eight thousand people on a waiting list to join. Their members are mostly in New York, Los Angeles, and Chicago, and hail from companies like Google, IBM, HBO, Chobani, Walmart, Visa, Doctors Without Borders, and *The New York Times.*

IT'S ALL ABOUT COMMUNITY

One of Chief's major benefits is their curated "Core Groups," which is made up of eight to ten executive female members who meet on a monthly basis, and it is designed to help forge connection and bonds to help. In one interview on hearing stories from members, Lindsay explains that in just a few Core sessions, "They feel seen and heard for the first time in their careers." Lindsay shared, "with so few female executives, they are surrounded by people who don't look or sound like them, and will never be one of the boys regardless of how well they get on with their male colleagues."

"Women leaders who connect with each other, do so deeply. The relationships can be so much more powerful because that feeling of being an only."

—LINDSAY KAPLAN, CHIEF

I've heard the same thing from Rachel Thomas, CEO and cofounder at Lean In, along with Sheryl Sandberg. The two created Lean In, a network aimed at women at all levels in the workplace. Rachel shared that when Lean In Circles were first introduced and women had permission to connect and share their experiences at work, it was a revelation. "Women felt validated, they weren't alone in their experience," Rachel explained. "It wasn't only them. Others were encountering similar issues as women executives." That shared understanding first allowed women to recognize they are not alone, then gave them collective power and access to mentoring, and the skills to do something about it. Rachel continued, "Since 2012, more than fifty thousand Lean In Circles have been created in nearly 190 countries." There is clearly a need for women to connect, share, and support one another.

Another conversation I had was with Kristy Wallace. She is the CEO at Ellevate Network, which has thousands of women members worldwide. They are changing the culture of business for women and underserved populations, not only because of their strength in numbers and the support they provide, but also how they run their organization as a certified B Corp.

Talking with Kristy inspired me greatly. She told me she testified in front of Congress last year regarding the plight of small businesses, and she is a persuasive figure with an enormous heart. Her work at Ellevate is about helping women move forward in the workplace, be it as business owners or business leaders, "Not everyone wants to be a manager or a CEO, but I think everyone wants to do meaningful work, and be recognized, and compensated." I'd always been impressed by how they focused on building community, and a greater vision for what women working together can achieve. Kristy told me they are "about helping our community to tap into a vision for themselves, and to achieve it. Then looking at the collective power of this community to create greater systemic change in the world, and in our society."

Speaking from my experience, I didn't take building a network really seriously until about ten years ago when I turned thirty-five. The evidence Herminia presented in my case was all true. My network was deeply imbedded into the companies I worked for and was a massive help in my ability to do an excellent job. However, in terms of my external network—from asking for advice, to finding new partners, and now fundraising for my organization—I felt like I had to start from scratch. I had witnessed firsthand how my husband's network swelled as we settled into life in Silicon Valley. He was always making connections and seemed to have an endless number of Starbucks meetings. It was his example that showed me I needed to be proactive and networking was a critical part of my job. A simple coffee meeting once a week became a mainstay for me. Meeting new people led to fresh ideas. I got better at asking for help, and it was always fun.

In talking with many successful women, I learned those who were most successful often had a key group of women who helped them. A good friend of mine, Obi Felten—Head of Getting Moonshots Ready for Contact with the Real World at X (Alphabet's moonshot factory)—recounted a beautiful story to me about her experience. Management expert and author, Nilofer Merchant, had invited her to join an informal network of women in the Bay Area when she first arrived from Europe. Before the rise of women's social networks, Nilofer had taken up the role herself. She set up a mailing list, which began with ten to twelve people and is still going today with a tight-knit group of fifty to sixty women. They would have an event once a quarter: brunch at someone's house one time, hiking another. It was a simple but effective way to connect and help each other.

Obi told me she had quickly realized that the women who had made it in Silicon Valley were all extraordinary because it's such a tough environment, and unless you had a phenomenal amount of grit and ability, you weren't going to make it. The group became crucial to Obi.

I had heard about informal networks like these throughout my career, but I could not be part of them. In hindsight, I wish I had the idea like Nilofer and created my own. I know so many women who would have benefitted. Now with my work at The Coaching Fellowship, creating community among our women social impact leaders is a critical component. Things are changing.

It's been a thrill to see an explosion of women's networks for various career levels and needs thrive. In talking with Lindsay, Kristy, and Rachel, I have heard so many stories of women getting the help they need and then giving back to the community. The virtuous circles women create now have more vehicles in place to authentically connect and empower one another forward. Connection is a first step to taking progress into our own hands. It's fantastic to know an entire new generation of women will now start their careers with access to other successful women in ways that have never been possible before.

What to Take Away?

Women networks are getting bigger and more pervasive and with that, we have the greatest of potential. With more ways to easily communicate, share experiences, and support one another across the globe, the power engine of women empowering women is not only rising but roaring.

#Do

One of the most powerful things you can do is teach the importance of network to a young woman in your world. Networks build over time, so the earlier one begins, the more valuable and extensive the network can become. Invite a young woman for a chat, suggest she meet others, and make introductions for her. Herminia shared the importance of being intentional and making time for those "strategic" connections and personal ones. Why not suggest she creates a weekly habit to meet someone new each week? It's an easy commitment and can quickly create impact.

#Do

Don't hold back. There's a belief that when we make it, we need to have things buttoned up, but that display of power and accomplishment doesn't show the whole picture. Young women leaders who only see success and do not hear the stories behind the success, may not see themselves as leadership material. Worse still, they may not have the courage to ask women leaders for advice and support. Be real and accessible like Lindsay wherever possible. There is strength in telling things as they are. Life is glorious and messy. Where possible, share your journey, share your struggles, and the example you show will become their standard.

#Remember

Kristy from Ellevate explained, its "relationship building which truly transforms society." We only have to think back to the days of small towns where everyone knew each other. If you needed something, someone would tell you where to go. It was the fabric of our neighborhoods and ultimately, still is. Building connections is the lifeblood of humanity. It is something we can and should do every day. So don't stop investing in your own network and connections. The more you do, the more you will be able to help everyone who comes later.

CHAPTER 3

PLANTING SEEDS
ON A ROCK

Where there is ruin, there is hope for a treasure.

—RUMI

The year after September 11, the world was in uproar. Toni Maloney was in Geneva at the United Nations Symposium with seven hundred other women all asking themselves, "What could they do as women to broker peace?" At the event, there had been a gathering led by twenty-five women representing the largest religions in the world, all coming together to pray for peace. In Toni's words, while praying was all well and good, "In my opinion that just wasn't going to get the job done fast enough!"

That's the type of woman Toni is—a native New Yorker, a "let's get this done" kind of lady, now in her early seventies. From my conversation with Toni on one November morning, she struck me as the likely ringleader who had led a contingent of these women at the United Nations Symposium directly to the hotel bar to figure what could be done.

Toni recalled asking, "What if business had a real role to play in peace, and what if we tried to work with women business owners and help them try to grow? What if that could get to real change?" Wherever you are in the world, if you cannot get access to skills and education, then you are at a significant disadvantage. Helping these women could create a deep and lasting impact. It would also go a long way to building understanding and partnerships across the world at a challenging time.

Five New York businesswomen came back home to New York City and founded the organization Bpeace (The Business Council for Peace), which focused on enabling women business owners, particularly in war-torn and developing countries. Their website says, "More jobs mean less violence." Women didn't have a voice in communities like Afghanistan and Rwanda where they initially began working. Bpeace learned though, if the women had economic clout, they could have a voice, and with money as a lever there would be a seat at the table for them. If Bpeace could help the women grow their business, create jobs, and gain more wealth, the cumulative impact would lead to real transformation in their communities. And maybe, a chance at peace.

Toni and her colleagues were way ahead of the trend. According to conflict prevention research from Inclusive Security in 2016, nations with higher levels of social, economic, and political gender equality are more stable and less likely to rely on military force to settle disputes. In the almost-twenty years that have passed since Bpeace was founded, a lot of good progress has happened. The United Nations Security Council Resolution 1325 on women, peace, and security was unanimously adopted to bring women into the peace process. Furthermore, the UN also established the Sustainable Economic Development Goals (SDGS), with Goal 5 being squarely focused on achieving gender equality and empowering all women and girls as a necessary foundation for a peaceful, prosperous, and sustainable world.

The World Bank now regularly reviews the state of female entrepreneurs and women in the global workforce, and why that matters for everyone's prosperity. Most recently, in 2020, as reported by USAID, the White House kicked off the Women's Global Development and Prosperity (W-GDP) Initiative aiming to reach fifty million women in the developing world by 2025 to enhance opportunities for women to participate meaningfully in the economy and advance national security. From governments around the world to our global governing bodies, it's clear they see the critical link between women's economic empowerment, and the prosperity and security of all people in the world.

It takes a village to raise a child, and players both big and small are needed to bring about systemic change. During the years Toni and Bpeace have been operating, they have played a significant role, bringing job creation and hope to tens of thousands of families across the world. In the early days, they were primarily focused on helping Afghan women. There was a sincere outpouring of support from US-based businesswomen queuing up to be mentors to their sisters in the Middle East. But for Bpeace mentors—"Skillanthropists," as they are called—bringing any sense of pity for the women they had signed up to support was quickly quashed. The Afghan women were strong, enduring business owners who did not need a beneficiary or to be treated as poor women. In many ways, their suffering had hardened their resolve. In post-conflict settings, studies like those by Elisabeth Rehn and Ellen Johnson Sirleaf from 2002 on the role of women in peace-building, women can bear both the economic and family responsibilities, particularly when the men in local communities may have been killed or disabled.

In developing and conflict-laden countries, women face an uphill battle, not only to build a thriving business, but from family pressure at home. If they started a business as a young woman, as soon as they get married, their in-laws mostly want them to stop working and take care of the home and children. If they stay in business, they are often subject to harassment and threats.

Alas, the costs of women giving up their businesses could be disastrous, says private sector development expert Carmen Niethammer, "Investing in women's economic participation, including through entrepreneurship, is often crucial for the stability of already fragile economies of conflict-affected societies." One cannot help but be humbled and astounded by the resoluteness of women building and rebuilding their countries. Not only providing food for their family's table but also resurrecting their economies and holding steadfast the path to peace.

SKILLS AND EDUCATION BRING SIGNIFICANT ADVANTAGES

Toni shared with me there are currently more than four hundred Bpeace "Skillanthropists" from fourteen countries who volunteer as advisors to women business owners across the globe. Toni explained, often the business challenges they would encounter were simplistic and naive, but she points out for example that after decades of war, Afghan women were learning how to run a business from scratch with no one to pass down advice and support. The mentors would introduce new ideas, methodologies, and procedures, and the business women brought their local knowledge—and that's how the magic happened.

Toni remembered the first time she introduced the concept of a Human Resource department and policies to Afghan women. They were blown away, "They would say you mean I don't have to hire my nephew's nephew for this job? You mean I can fire my nephew's nephew?" You don't always know what you need, and that gap of not knowing is crucial. This sharing of knowledge and skills struck me as so simple. It costs little to share an hour of our time and expertise each month. Yet that could be the difference between a business surviving or failing, potentially once again creating economic instability and increased violence.

My connection to Toni had been through my mentor, coach, and board member to The Coaching Fellowship, Athena Katsaros. She had joined as a Skillanthropist in 2005. Only a few months later, on one chilly December morning, she had found herself in Kabul, Afghanistan ready to teach a day-long class to 130 Afghan businesswomen, most of whom owned their own business. As a stark reminder of the challenges they faced daily, Athena arrived at the location to find no electricity, no lights, and no heating. Thankfully, someone was sent to find a generator and was successful. Athena recalled it was still colder inside than it was outside. They all kept their coats and scarves on.

She remembers several women in the audience were wearing burkas. Other women were in modest, dark business attire with long jackets that went down to their knees and loose scarves on their heads to cover their hair. Athena had mused at the time, "What must they be thinking as they wait to see what this tall, blond American businesswoman is going to teach them?"

Thanks to a group of translators, Athena taught a visioning and planning tool she had developed called the "Success Map." The basic idea was that if you want to get somewhere, you need a map to help guide you. In a series of teaching moments and small group work that day, Athena helped the women from all types of businesses and backgrounds think about the future they wanted to create in their business and how to get there.

Reflecting on their strengths and skills and on what options, opportunities, and resources were available to them—plus locking in who was going to help them achieve their goal—they all successfully created a twelve-month vision and planning document for their business. A big step forward in strategic thinking and goal setting, something they had rarely done before. Athena shared, "What a number of the

Afghan businesswomen told me that day was that they had not allowed themselves to have a vision for the future of their businesses before. Their lives had been so uncertain after years of war that they were not used to dreaming about the future. I saw their faces light up when they envisioned what they could create and I realized the power, and importance of imagination."

After a few years of successfully helping Afghan women with access to business skills, the US State Department—who Bpeace had been working with—were asked if they could do the same for Afghan men. They had just wanted to help women, but when they asked the Afghan women what they thought, they said yes of course because unless you help the men, we're never going to achieve anything we want as a country. Bpeace decided to only work with male-owned businesses that empowered women inside their business, providing jobs and putting women in leadership positions. The truth is, we need all people to be enabled so that more can come forward and more people can thrive.

ASHES CAN BE FERTILE SOIL

It was through Toni that I got to meet Fereshteh Forough, founder of Code to Inspire and Building Afghanistan 2.0. Fereshteh is an example of an Afghan businesswoman who Toni was hoping to see manifest from their work. She has built a successful organization teaching young Afghan girls to code. I had not expected to be moved to tears in my interview with Fereshteh. Although I will admit it was not the first time I had cried in one of my interviews, and it would not be the last. The work of writing this book you hold in your hands has definitely been one of heart and soul.

Fereshteh has a wisdom and presence of a woman who knows the world. Currently in her mid-thirties, she is too young to have experienced such hardship. She was born a refugee; her family having fled Western Afghanistan to Iran as the Soviets invaded. It's clear the circumstances of her upbringing have forged her tenacity and a natural way to make things work on her own.

> ## "I learned the value of entrepreneurship from my Mom, who proved that in life great things can start with empty hands."
>
> —FERESHTEH FOROUGH

She was one of eight children, living on food stamps and secondhand clothes. Her mom had become a seamstress and brought in much-needed cash. Fereshteh humbly explained it was this extra money that allowed her mom to invest in her education and finish high school.

What touches me as I talk with Fereshteh is her positive and joyful attitude and her way of being perhaps, forged from such adversity that she finds the gift in all things. At one point, she shares her favorite Rumi quote, "Where there is ruin, there is hope for a treasure." While her upbringing appears to have been impoverished with little in the way of luxuries, she loved school and was smart. Her motivation was learning—where she was always at the top of the class—and she took pride and fulfillment in that.

Fereshteh and her family moved back to Afghanistan in 2002, one year after the fall of the Taliban, a country ravaged by decades of war and ruin. She had been struck by the scarce opportunities for women in her homeland, "It was hard being a woman in Afghanistan, it was a different world for me because in Iran I had more freedom." I had to pause in our interview for a second to let that sink in. That Iran was like a "free" place compared to her home. It was that sense of freedom that had pushed Fereshteh to blaze her own path.

She was outspoken and hungry to grow. When she got into computer science, she had chosen the farthest edge of what was possible in Afghanistan for a woman. Fereshteh shares, "that really made me a target of hate, there were threats and pushback." It was a rare subject for women to study anywhere at the time, but she had the foresight that this could not only be her ticket for a better life, but it could also be one for thousands more women and girls in her country. "Most families prefer their daughters become a teacher as it's a respected, well-paying job where women only work with other women," Fereshteh explained. She tells me that with the internet, geographical boundaries didn't matter, you could walk around the world virtually, thus, more freely. No one was going to tell you what to do, harass you, or ask for your papers.

"The most important thing for women is that they can earn money, and gain financial independence. Then they can choose whatever they want to do, and they can become a decision-maker in their community or in their family. I saw that was possible and wanted to empower that in women," says Fereshteh. Her self-determination had earned her a bachelor's degree in computer science in Afghanistan, then a scholarship to do her masters at The Technical University of Berlin, Germany. A place she loved and where she herself became a professor for three years teaching computer science.

When she returned to Afghanistan, Fereshteh worked as a professor at Herat University until she faced major threats from extremists. She moved to the US in 2012 and has lived in New York City ever since. A teacher at her core, she longed to make a difference back home. In 2015, Fereshteh took all of her experiences and wishes for the world and opened a coding school—the first of its kind—for girls in Herat, Afghanistan. All while sitting at her laptop in Brooklyn, she founded Code to Inspire, providing young Afghan women programming skills to empower and inspire them toward financial and social independence.

Her teaching platform has places for fifty young girls who attend the school for a one-year period, learning everything from web design to JavaScript, Mobile App development, and other coding skills. She hoped these critical skills would translate into job opportunities, and proudly told me, three hundred girls have graduated so far: 60 percent have found jobs within their community using skills they learned, and 10 percent have become entrepreneurs creating their own technology start-ups. Furthermore, some of those young women are now earning double or triple of their male family members. The average 2021 salary in Afghanistan continues to be around $150 per month according to Salary Explorer.

The successes of the girls at Code to Inspire are riveting, like a young girl who was one of the first students. Her English was poor, she wasn't good at math or logic, and she had never touched a computer before. When asked what her motivation was to learn to code, she determinedly proclaimed she wanted to make money, and there was absolutely nothing wrong with that! She came from a challenging financial background and couldn't even afford to pay the few cents bus fare to the school, which Code to Inspire offered to sponsor. The girl was strong-willed and a sharp student. She learned English quickly and became one of their best students. A month after graduating, she got back in touch to excitedly share she had convinced a company to hire her at $200 per month to build their website and bring them online. It was her first job and she was making more money than anyone else in her family.

Time again there were examples like this that with encouragement and access to resources, the young girls would create their own opportunities and begin investing first in themselves, then their communities. In Fereshteh's mind, it was all about providing equal resources. "There is potential in girls, but you have to give them the skills and resources to bloom." At another moment in my interview, I was again brought to tears when Fereshteh explained that her work had been like "planting seeds on a rock," but with all that struggle and hardship and the willingness of the girls to try, just like her mother, she had made something out of empty hands.

The road had not been an easy one. Fereshteh was threatened, she had to fight through backlash, and endure the struggles every entrepreneur must face—funding, resources, and keeping her business alive. Due to travel limitations, she tells me she hasn't been able to visit her family for eight years. She shared, "there were many times I cried and wanted to give up. Then, I think of the girls who are going to school with bare feet in Afghanistan's mountains. I thought of those girls who sit outside during the hot summer, in the rain and snow to learn, and to change their lives. I can only fight for those girls through the power of the internet, and through the safety of my refugee status that keeps me so painfully far away."

Of the biggest problems Afghan women are still facing, says Najla Ayubi from a 2010 report from the Asian Foundation, is education with illiteracy topping the list. According to Human Rights Watch, "sixteen years after the US-led military intervention that ousted the Taliban government, an estimated two-thirds of Afghan girls do not go to school," and among adult women, "only 19 percent are literate compared to 49 percent of adult men." That's why the work of Toni and Fereshteh, and others seeking to provide access to key skills, is so critical. With knowledge and power, women can increase their job opportunities, and they can advocate for their own equal rights.

Fereshteh isn't stopping here. When Venture Beat's Dean Takahashi asked her about her future goals for Code to Inspire back in 2019, she replied, "every day I get messages and emails from girls asking me when we're going to open more schools in other cities. In the longer term, it's about empowering women in developing countries and underprivileged communities. If I can do something in Afghanistan—which to some people is an impossible place, a war zone—I'll be able to do that in any other part of the world."

Fereshteh told me it's the girls and the sisterhood environ-ment she created within the school that makes all the hard-ship bearable. "I want the girls to know it's vital to support each other, and create a culture where they feel secure and celebrated. It's about a sense of belonging where I take your hand and help you get to a position, so that then we can take another woman's hand. It becomes a loop, where everyone is connected." And everyone can help a woman forward.

There it is again, the idea of the virtuous circle, of women empowering women. From all across the world, from New York to Herat, women are finding ways big and small to make this the time of women. My only wish is that we can get the flywheel spinning faster because I know that if we can plant a seed on a rock, and that flower will still bloom, then there are orchards of fruit waiting to be planted too.

What to Take Away?

In talking with Toni from Bpeace, I have been struck by how much knowledge is missing in the world and by the possibilities of what could change if more power was held in the hands of more women.

#Remember

Take the story of the Afghan woman who didn't know she didn't have to hire her nephew's nephew. It seems obvious to us, but we don't always know what we don't know. Be aware that often the basics are what people just starting out are looking for, and there's no shame in that. Furthermore, whenever you are explaining or teaching, double-check "did she get all that?" Create a safe space where she feels she can ask you to elaborate. Helping each other learn without shame is powerful.

#Do

There is much to say on the topic of mentoring. What I want to impart here is that you can be a mentor regardless of your age, position, and experience. We all have something to offer when it comes to skill building and advice. Offering to be someone's mentor is a courageous and bold act. It doesn't need to be something you do every week or even consistently with the same person. Offering advice to many women at varying levels and intervals can be transformative and manageable for you too.

#Reflect

I hope you were as inspired as I was by Fereshteh and her beautiful story of "planting a seed on a rock." It took bravery and tenacity, but it also required a belief that this was the right thing to do. Even if we think we have little to offer, fortune does indeed favor the brave. So let's push for what's important, and take a stand for planting as many seeds as possible!

CHAPTER 4

TAKING ON GIANTS

———

We cannot change what we are not aware of,
and once we are aware,
we cannot help but change.

—SHERYL SANDBERG

Poking your finger into the face of major technology companies like Google, Facebook, and Microsoft with all their money and might is not for the faint of heart. But small actions can become bold steps. Tracy Chou, software engineer and now a diversity activist, did just that. She set out to shine a light on the dismal numbers of women in technology. Within weeks, the twenty-seven-year-old second-generation Taiwanese American was catapulted into the media spotlight as the face of Silicon Valley's diversity problem. Everyone was talking about her and it.

According to Salvador Rodriguez from The International Business Times, Fortune 500 companies, as well as the latest

Sand Hill Road funded "bro" start-up companies, are sorely lacking in representation of women and minorities. Data back from 2014, released by tech companies feeling pressured by Tracy blowing the whistle on their lack of diversity, painted a discouraging picture. As reported by Lisa Eadicicco of Business Insider, Google, LinkedIn, and more show only around 37 percent of their workforce as being women and, appallingly, just 17 percent for numbers of women in tech. Start-ups were just as bad, if not worse, as one 2018 BBC article explained, with the likes of Uber being well-known for their unwelcoming culture to downright open discrimination of women.

Since the 1970s when technology as a profession was expanding, the number of women in computing had been steadily growing, even reaching a high of 36 percent for women in tech in 1991, as Sage Lazzaro from *The Observer* catalogued in 2017. Then, the trend started reversing and declining downward. When I hit the Valley in 2009, that was all plainly obvious to me as I found a desert of women in technical roles. You just had to look around the office or in the line for morning coffee at Starbucks. Eighty percent were male.

TRACY TOOK NOTICE

That's what had piqued Tracy's interest. In October 2013, she attended the annual Grace Hopper Celebration of Women in Computing conference, which was designed to bring research and career interests of women in computing to the fore. It was also the world's largest gathering of women in computing.

Tracy—well-accustomed to being the "only" woman in computing—explained to Nathan Heller for *Vogue* magazine, that at the time she had become ever more curious about female representation in technology companies and decided to gather data to assess the severity of the issue. Unbeknownst to her, she had lit the touch paper at the same time.

Tracy graduated from the prestigious Stanford University with a degree in Electrical Engineering with a concentration on computer software, followed by a Masters in Computer Science. She specialized in machine learning and artificial intelligence.

She shared this with me as our interview started. We Zoomed from her London apartment, where she has been marooned since February, unable to travel back to the USA since the start of the COVID-19 pandemic. In talking about her background, I was surprised to learn both her parents were software engineers and scientists. They came to the United States to get their PhDs and decided to stay and work in technology.

"My mom was a software engineer and even growing up I would hear her stories of how she was treated, especially compared to my dad. It was so easy to see the blatant discrimination as they had the same educational background, the same PhDs from the same university, and they were in America right at the same time," she explained.

Tracy said she figured this was "just the way the world was run," and that hearing these stories in her upbringing was normal. She told Jessi Hempel at *Wired* that she, too, had gone to university to study engineering, and was not surprised at all to find that she was one of only three women out of fifty students in class.

"This is kind of what I expected." Tracy told me, and at the same time, she was still disappointed she didn't fit in.

I had known Tracy for several years; she had been a coaching fellow at The Coaching Fellowship during her first year of managing and maximizing her newfound fame as a diversity activist. The media attention and responsibility on her young shoulders was immense, and I observed how she continued on with grace, care, and determination. Tracy exudes calm, intelligence, and intention. She is passionate and driven and also incredibly thoughtful. She is an open book, willing to share her personal journey and struggles publicly.

If the seeds of her gendered experiences of computer science had been sown at home and at university, then they were fed and watered, and grew large at her first job out of college at Quora. The start-up was a crowdsourced question-and-answer platform that launched in 2009. It hit the fast lane a few years later when it received $226 million in venture funding, reported Shoshanna Delventhal at Investopedia. Tracy was the only female software engineer when she joined Quora and was often miserable. She shared that initially she thought her colleagues' behavior around her was because she was a recent graduate or because her undergraduate degree was in electrical engineering. Tracy casually dropped into the conversation that although she had graduated in the top 5 percent of her class, in her mind, she hadn't thought about it being systemic gender bias. It was more about her than them. Over time, as the incidents mounted, she wised up and could clearly see it for the standard, garden-variety sexism, misogyny, and gaslighting that it was.

In a 2018 interview that Tracy did with Rachel Gutman at *The Atlantic,* she described how throughout her early career, her colleagues made it clear that they saw work as a place to find romantic partners. She went on to explain that people would say things like, "'Wow, you're so cute,' and would make me feel as if it were a novelty that I was even there." At times during her early years in Silicon Valley, Tracy recalled crying herself to sleep each night and wondering if she should be in software. She had found her passion though. She loved coding and building things from the ground up. It was worth fighting for, and she thought maybe she could change the sexist culture. Tracy showed her willingness to speak up early on and raised issues around being treated differently as a woman with her teams.

"I was told that the sexism did not exist, and because I believed there was sexism, that I was projecting, and seeing it around me where it didn't exist."

—TRACY CHOU

Maybe, it was only in her mind, Tracy mused. I remember thinking the same thing myself when I arrived in the Valley and was trying hard to fit in as the only female director-level executive. Over the years, I'd hear more colleagues say the same thing. Just as Tracy had, women will look internally for the root of a problem, and men will look externally for the answer.

WHEN YOU TAKE SMALL BOLD BRAVE STEPS

Tracy joined Pinterest, the pinboard company, in 2011, becoming one of the first fifteen employees. There she focused on growing her engineering career. Pinterest was booming and was an exciting place to be. Tracy admitted to me she had been burned by her previous experiences, and she was more than happy to work at a place that was not toxic. A place where she could focus on what she loved doing.

Then came an opportunity to go to the Grace Hopper conference for female engineers in 2013. People were bemoaning, as usual, the lack of diversity in tech. Being the engineer she was, Tracy decided to survey the numbers more closely for herself. However, there was little data to go on. Tracy explained, "The numbers which were being banded around were actually far lower than anyone wanted to admit." At the conference, Facebook COO Sheryl Sandberg was recorded by Miranda Katz at *Wired* saying the number of women in tech was dropping. In a 2016 Techies feature, Tracy explained what she had thought in response, "How do you know what the numbers are? How does anyone know what the numbers are?" In an industry that was so data driven, obsessed with dashboards and metrics so that everything could be tracked, and understood and improved, there was no data on diversity.

"We need to work together to make that happen, and it starts with having honest dialogues about how we're actually doing, as an industry, to encourage women in computing. So, where are the numbers?"

—TRACY CHOU

This led to her now-famous 2013 Medium blog post, "Where are the numbers?" She called for collective transparency to get the "real data" and understand the severity of the issue. Tracy's idea was to get a baseline that could be referenced to see how well the industry was doing. To get things started, and with her employer's blessing, she released the number of women in technical roles at Pinterest was just 12 percent and called for other companies to report their data on her public spreadsheet. It hit an immediate nerve.

Within a week, Tracy's repository on GitHub—an online platform for version control mainly used by software developers—had data for over fifty companies, and by April 2016, over two hundred tech companies had self-reported their female employee data. Smaller start-ups had initially begun reporting, then, as Jessi Hempel at *Wired* shared in 2015, "Larger start-ups like Etsy (nineteen of 149), Dropbox (twenty-five of 275), and Airbnb (eighteen of 143) joined in." Finally, the storm Tracy had set in motion forced larger and more established tech companies like Facebook, Google, and Microsoft to come clean. It became glaringly clear across the entire tech industry that it was exactly as white and male as everyone had suspected. The numbers were both unsurprising and devastating, but that didn't matter. What mattered more was that Tracy had established a mechanism that still stands to this day. Diversity reports are published by tech companies annually, and display how women and minorities are faring in technology roles and leadership.

Public diversity reports have become routine, and they go a long way to shedding light on progress or lack thereof. By having to be transparent, there has been some accountability for companies to make progress on diversity issues. I recall working at Mozilla in 2015 and being part of the first "DEI" (Diversity Equity and Inclusion) Working Group. The initiative had been started by Mitchell Baker, the Chairwoman and cofounder of Mozilla, and was deeply supported and championed by the CEO, Chris Beard. Others, as Sam Sabin at Morning Consult reported in 2020, also took note, like "Facebook investing in a number of computer science education programs. Apple creating the Apple HBCU Scholars Program, a leadership, and internship program for students at historically black colleges and universities. Microsoft working with several outside organizations to fix the talent 'pipeline' problem and get more under-represented people interested in tech careers."

Six years after Tracy's efforts, the industry however, still appears to be moving at a glacial pace when it comes to representation. For example, Megan Rose Dickey at TechCrunch quotes Google's Diversity reports showing in 2014 it was 61.3 percent white and 69.4 percent male. Fast-forward to today and the latest available numbers (2019) for Google is 54.4 percent white and 68.4 percent male. It's clear more needs to be done, and Tracy is at the forefront of change, only this time with more allies.

THE FUTURE IS MORE INCLUSIVE

Today, Tracy is one of eight female partners who founded Project Include, a nonprofit setting out to speed up the stalled process of diversifying companies. Her esteemed colleagues include Ellen Pao, who filed an unsuccessful gender discrimination lawsuit against her venture capital employer, Kleiner Perkins, and spent several years in court highlighting the technology industry's lack of diversity.

Ellen became interim CEO of Reddit, a controversial social news aggregation and discussion website, where she was eventually ousted for making decisions that banned revenge porn and other controversial Reddit communities who, as reported by The Guardian's Beth Winegarner in 2015, fostered attacks on women, overweight people, and minorities. Locked out of their favorite forums, angry Reddit users called her "Chairman Pao," and compared her to Adolf Hitler. More than 213,000 users signed a petition for Ellen to be ousted. The backlash she received while seeking to stop harassment highlighted both the treatment of women leaders in technology and the desire to keep the status quo.

Tracy shared that their main aim at Project Include is to support technology companies in assessing where they are lacking in inclusion, then help them develop plans to create change while holding those in leadership accountable. Quoted in Rachel Gutman's 2018 article in *The Atlantic,* Tracy explained, "most leaders at these tech companies are men. If they can see themselves succeeding, and they can see other people like themselves, they don't really find it to be a problem that women aren't there." Tracy doesn't stop there. She also founded Block Party, an app that targets online harassment by giving people a safer experience online and protecting them from bullying and abuse. She is an unstoppable force.

Tracy did not set out to be an activist. She took a simple, but provocative step to shed light on an issue felt by her personally, her friends, and women across Silicon Valley. Her actions sent ripples through the entire tech industry. As reported by Investing News Network in 2020, an industry so large that five of the top ten US companies by market cap are all technology companies. Known collectively as FAAMG, an abbreviation coined by Goldman Sachs for the five top-performing tech stocks: Facebook, Amazon, Apple, Microsoft, Google, their impact and influence on every aspect of our lives is immeasurable. Isn't it important therefore that companies of this magnitude and power are built and run by a diverse group of people with all perspectives taken into consideration? This thinking had led her to go further, bring allies, and find more ways to solve this pervasive and critically important problem.

Her activism has come with its challenges. Tracy has had several stalkers—one who is "persistent and dedicated" in London—and she worries constantly that someone is following her. "I'm always thinking, can my geolocation information be leaked? Do I have my phone ready to go to call people in case something bad happens?"

She keeps her Metropolitan Police Report ID number close by so her file can be accessed quickly if, God forbid, she needs to make an emergency call. She also shared that she experienced harassment in London during the pandemic, including being yelled at to go back to China (she is from California). It tore at my heart as she recounted her stories, but she tells me it strengthens her resolve to find more ways to support women and minorities.

In a 2020 Marker article, Tracy explained how she has been sexually harassed, threatened, and stalked. "I have had different investors inquire about my age, and relationship status, and tell me about their first-time having sex. In a room full of men, I have been completely ignored and talked over, despite being the expert." She describes her encounters as her entrepreneurial endurance training.

As disturbing as this is, many women are subject to similarly blatant forms of discrimination and harassment. Others experience death by a thousand cuts, where discrimination and harassment are present but just under the surface enough not to be addressed or corrected. Early in my career, like many young women, I experienced unwanted sexual advances. At the time, I feared my rebuke might harm my career. In the workplace, women experience a range of situations, comments, attacks, and behavior that are at best uncomfortable and at worst dangerous or career-killing.

Reflecting on what we face in the workplace, it makes me think just how much stronger we are as women, for all we have already endured in both the big and small ways. That's a power to be recognized and unleashed in ourselves and in others.

How does Tracy continue her great and necessary work despite her personal risk?

The 2020 Marker interview continued, "People ask me if it's worth it to put myself through all the pain and suffering. But how could I not? I'm one of the few that has the privilege to try. I am immensely lucky to be able to do what I do. And the crucible of my experiences makes me uniquely suited and determined to solve these problems." I think again about the simple action she took back in 2013 and the storm she created. It not only galvanized thousands of people to take up the diversity in tech mantle, it also galvanized Tracy, her role, her commitment, and her place in the world. Who knows where our actions lead? If we don't try, then millions of women could be missing out on the change you could make.

What to Take Away?

Tracy did not set out to become an activist and household name, but she had a bold set of beliefs, was brave, and chose to live her life according to her values. Perhaps, that means something was eventually bound to happen. I agree more with Seneca when he said two thousand years ago, "Luck is what happens when preparation meets opportunity."

#Remember

Small actions matter. Step by step by step. We read the story of Tracy, and we see a bold and influential step. Every small action is worth taking. We never fully know the ripple effects of a piece of advice we gave, a connection we made, a reference we wrote. The step is meaningful in itself, and the potential is boundless.

#Do

Share what you know or don't know as broadly as possible. Your ideas, insights, and perspectives cannot catch on if people can't hear you. Often asking others for help is a way to drive attention. People want to help, given an opportunity to contribute, so tell people what you need, give them a way to engage, and let them help you.

#Reflect

Play to your strengths. Tracy is a computer scientist; she loves data and math. She focused on unearthing diversity data partly because that's the world she understood and lived every day. It was also the language Silicon Valley spoke and deeply resonated with the engineers who saw an easy way to participate. Ask yourself what your strengths are, what comes easy to you, and how that could help a sister. Are you a writer, a cheerleader? Do you like to say the hard things, or are you more often a voice to confide in? Knowing and using what you are innately good at is your best advantage.

CHAPTER 5

GIRLS RISING

——

Little girls with dreams become women with vision.

—UNKNOWN

One hundred and thirty-two million girls didn't go to school today, according to UNICEF in 2021. Not because they didn't want to go, but because they didn't have the chance. Without an education, girls around the world remain impoverished, unable to advocate for themselves, and—as USAID stated in 2018—the world misses out on the opportunity their success and impact could bring for improved health, sustained peace, and economic growth. When we think about a future where women are equal, it requires our girls to have every opportunity to thrive and grow because it's pretty hard for them to dream when they don't even know what's possible.

In 2021, UNICEF explained that the main reasons for girls being out of school in the developing world range from lack of hygiene or sanitation needs of girls, to long and unsafe commutes to school, to poor families favoring investing in a son's education over their daughters, to extreme poverty, war, child marriage, and sexual violence.

The numbers are insurmountable: a 2016 Global Women's Institute reports approximately sixty million girls are sexually assaulted on their way to or at school every year. On March 8, 2021, International Women's Day, UNICEF went on to report that one hundred million girls are at risk of child marriage in the next decade. April 2020 data from the Malala Fund estimates that with 90 percent of the world's schools shuttered, twenty million more secondary school-age girls could be out of school by the end of the COVID-19 pandemic.

IT'S NOT ALWAYS A STRAIGHT LINE

These numbers are not new to me. I took part in the Nike Foundation's Girl Effect Accelerator in collaboration with the Unreasonable Group back in 2014, a first of its kind international accelerator dedicated exclusively to scaling up ventures that are measurably benefiting girls in poverty. I volunteered, along with my husband as a mentor and coach. Every day of the two-week program, I was shocked by the statistics and stories I learned: girls risking their lives working in brick factories in India, girls carrying rocks on their heads from quarries in Ethiopia, girls trafficked out of South Africa for sexual exploitation. Despite all the difficult conversations and realities we confronted as mentors supporting the entrepreneurs on the ground, the experience was one of the most rewarding for me by helping advance and give girls' issues voice and amplification.

At the event, I met a fellow mentor, Holly Gordon. She had taken the world by storm a year before by producing and launching the feature film, *Girl Rising*. The movie told the story of nine girls' lives in nine countries. It showed their everyday hardships and the pursuit of their dreams. The making of the film explains each girl had their story told by an acclaimed female writer from their country, and then their story was narrated by a famous actress such as Anne Hathaway, Priyanka Chopra, Meryl Streep, and more. The film had struck a deep chord. The website states it has been translated into thirty languages, aired multiple times in 170 countries to over two hundred million viewers, and helped ignite a global movement to support girls' education and equality. As the movie proclaims, "*Girl Rising* proves that one girl with courage is a revolution."

Holly and I reminisced about the Girl Effect Accelerator. It was now more than six years ago when we convened in Napa, California, with the inspiring entrepreneurs we helped support in their quest to empower girls. I had asked Holly if she would share her founding story with me and how had she come to create *Girl Rising*.

Holly had learned early in her life that she was a storyteller. A friend had landed a job to write an article about the last living tigers in the wild, and he invited her to join him in India. It was a love story, not with him but with writing. Realizing her talent and desire to tell important stories, she decided TV was a better medium with bigger budgets and focused her career toward television journalism.

Her first job was at ABC, working for the broadcast anchor Peter Jennings on *ABC World News Tonight*. It had been a great entry into the fast-paced news business. Holly shared, "I loved the news business. It was creative. It was constantly interesting. If you're a curious person, being a journalist is really like going to a candy store every day. And I thought I would spend my career rising through the ranks of ABC." During that time, she also fell in love, got married, and had two children. She wanted to be a superstar at ABC, but soon she felt the pressure of motherhood. With two little ones at home, she couldn't jump on a plane at a moment's notice or work in the office until the early hours to finish a story.

The breaking point came when she was asked to cover a coal mining accident in West Virginia. With miners still stuck underground, Holly faced being gone for at least three to four weeks. It was impossible. Economically, her husband made more money than she did, so it made sense for her to quit her beloved job and stay home. "I cried so hard. I was literally watching my dream crumble in front of me. I thought about what my mother told me. If I worked really hard, I could have everything, and I thought to myself, no you can't!"

Resilient, smart, and desperate to make an impact, she began working on stories and projects from home. One of those projects led her to the Tribeca Film Festival, where she connected with former ABC producer and Academy Award nominee, Tom Yellin (Emmys) at The Documentary Group, and they started working together. Holly told me Tom understood her and the pressures at home. He had built a successful company with really amazing smart women. Tom had a bunch of projects underway, including the girl's education project. Holly told Tom she thought they had something really special and there was a change in the world's appetite for transformational stories. *Girl Rising* was born.

The real stories behind success are never quite what you imagine. In Holly's case, her story is even more impactful. An ambitious and successful TV producer gives up her career for her family only to reinvent herself and start a global movement for girls' education and empowerment.

Holly had been an inspiration for us participating in The Girl Effect Accelerator, where at times it was easy to get depressed and despondent. As Daniel Epstein at The Unreasonable Group had explained while launching the program on their website in 2015, that less than two cents of every international development dollar goes to girls. It was an honor to mentor alongside her, and know change was being made. The ten entrepreneurs in the program were building strong, locally driven, and independent impactful businesses. They were all dedicated to positively benefiting millions of girls living in poverty.

THE STORY OF ZANAAFRICA

One of those memorable founders for Holly and I was Megan White Mukuria, founder of ZanaAfrica. Living in Kenya for seventeen years, her story and business had struck us deeply, mainly because we had never even considered the nature of her work—girls education in health, hygiene, and puberty. How completely naive we were to the basic needs of women and girls living on less than two dollars a day around the world.

While working with Kenyan street children in 2001, the ZanaAfrica website explains, Megan learned that sanitary pads were out of reach for 65 percent of girls in the country. According to Laura Begley Bloom's 2018 *Forbes* interview with Megan, two in three girls in Kenya must use homemade materials like rags to manage their periods, and as you might imagine they don't really work well. I recall her telling me that young girls in rural Kenya usually only have one pair of panties. It was heart-wrenching. They typically stay home from school one week in a month because of the stigma and lack of facilities to support menstruating girls. Even more shocking, in the same article from Laura Begley Bloom, Megan explained, "a recent study in Kenya showed that one in ten girls have engaged in transactional sex in order to obtain pads." Appalled by the situation, Megan did something about it.

She founded ZanaAfrica with the belief that sanitary pads and reproductive health education are a basic human right, and it gets to this lack of access being part of the root causes of gender inequality. First, she set about developing a radically cheap sanitary pad that was affordable to girls living on less than two dollars a day. Then she began tackling health education awareness and developing more affordable girl's health products like girls' underwear. They have supported more than fifty thousand girls by reducing the stigma of periods and promoting women's health throughout Kenya. Megan remains most proud of her work of girls staying in education, such as New Adventure School in Kibera, Nairobi, a former school she supported that called to let her know "that for the first time in their thirteen-year history, 100 percent of their girls had matriculated from seventh to eighth grade." Megan proudly said in a 2016 *Harvard Magazine* article with Olivia Campbell, "that was incredibly validating—to see girls' lives change so positively."

THE SURPRISING IMPACT OF INVESTING IN GIRLS' EDUCATION

Investing in girls' education can provide big returns, greater GDP, greater earning, and more lives saved. According to one 2018 USAID report, if 10 percent more adolescent girls attend school, a country's GDP increases by an average of 3 percent, and furthermore, an extra year of secondary school for girls can increase their future earnings by 10 to 20 percent. Even more poignant, a child whose mother can read is 50 percent more likely to live past the age of five. As One.org said in 2017, "all that for less than the cost of a loaf of bread each day, a girl in the world's poorest countries could go to school." To me that seems like a small expense that could quite literally change the world. When we think of taking progress into our own hands for women, it's easy to think we cannot make a difference, and here we can see it is virtually pennies that will change a girl's life forever.

"If you invest in a girl, she becomes a woman and she invests in everyone else."

—MELINDA GATES

That's the main work of Tammy Tibbetts, the cofounder of She's the First, a nonprofit that helps support girls' education and empowerment. In 2016, Tammy joined the Coaching Fellowship as one of our first fellows. Her impressive work had already stretched six years and supported thousands of girls to be the first in their family to go to school or college. What had started as a social media campaign in 2009 to raise awareness of the lack of education for girls, is now a multimillion-dollar organization that reaches more than 138,000 girls each year across twenty-six countries through their education programs and initiatives.

I interviewed Tammy in her New York apartment. As with every time I get the gift of speaking with her, I was overwhelmed by her passion and heart-forward way of being. She was only twenty-three when she began her work—a young girl herself—and she has grown ever more into an eloquent and inspirational voice for women and girls. Tammy argued, "as a global community, we must take action because when you educate a girl, there are untold positive benefits breaking the cycle of poverty. Helping her family, lifting up her community, and ultimately driving economic progress for everyone." Tammy has witnessed this impact with her own eyes time and again. More than a decade later, she now sees the women she helped thriving, supporting their local communities, and even building community-based organizations of their own.

One such example is Eliakunda Kaaya (Ellie) in Tanzania, who was a She's the First fellow. She put her success to full use by creating her own nonprofit organization—Her Journey to School—which supports girls in her home village. In a 2020 article for AfricAid by Alecia McClure, Ellie said, "In this community, being born female is a disadvantage and you have to fight for your right to an education. I feel responsible for other girls in my community who have gone through the same thing as me, or even worse scenarios. There are many girls dropping out of school because of pregnancy and the door to their education is being shut." Ellie's organization is working hard to change the status quo and her community's beliefs, which do not support girls' education. She is ambitiously promoting gender equality and helping those local girls stay in school and understand their rights.

Each time I hear a new story about girl's empowerment, I am struck by the continued and relentless desire of women to make things better for another, to ease the path, and hold up a light for more to follow. Tammy's organization's light now spans across eleven different countries, from East and West Africa to South Asia and Latin America. She shares that her work is not only helping girls go to and stay in school, but she is also working to design programs with girls' needs at the center, such as their partnership with MAIA Impact in Guatemala.

Indigenous girls are among the most marginalized in Guatemalan society, so they're the last in their families to be educated. "Fewer than 20 percent of Indigenous girls graduate from high school, and only 2 percent go on to university," MAIA Impact reports on their website. Spanish is the national language that is rarely spoken at home, but when these young girls go to school, they learn Spanish and become invaluable members of society. They are able to help read important documents and other necessary notices for the family. They translate important health messages to their communities, like the COVID-19 pandemic and public safety.

Tammy is proud that cultural stereotypes are shifting with more girls being educated and setting the example of what they're capable of.

One of the most important recent projects from She's the First has been to initiate and co-organize the Girls' Bill of Rights, a declaration of the rights all girls are entitled to. The document, which was presented at the United Nations in October 2019 on International Day of the Girl, had no precedent. NPR's Diane Cole explained in October 2019, inputs for the bill were gathered by more than one thousand girls from thirty-four countries submitting their rights in five languages. From there, a team of fifteen young women from across the globe worked via WhatsApp to synthesize the finds and produce the final document.

The bill of rights begins with the preface, "All girls have the right to...." From deserving equal opportunity to attending school all the way to graduation, to being free from discrimination, violence, and exploitation to access to health and sexual education, and being protected by the law in all matters. The NPR segment went on to explain, each of the ten rights were backed up by data from the UN, UNICEF, and the World Bank. So far the Bill has reached 150 million people, and the UN Secretary General has been asked how their voices will be incorporated into the greater UN agenda moving forward. How inspiring and fitting that change is being made for girls by girls.

The evidence is too important not to be told both in terms of the appalling losses and suffering of girls, but also the tremendous opportunities for them and the world when they are heard, taken care of, educated, and allowed to thrive. In their 2017 article for The Brookings Institution, Christina Kwauk and Amanda Braga call secondary schooling for girls the most cost-effective and best investment against climate change, and that girls' education reduces a country's vulnerability to natural disasters. Women appear to be the answer to most of the world's troubles in all the research I've done. There is no such thing as a silver bullet, but honestly, investing in girls seems to come pretty close.

As mothers, aunts, sisters, or friends, taking an early interest in the young girls in your life is a no-brainer. This is a gentle reminder to not take those moments for granted. You have no idea what and where your attention and teachings might go with her young mind. Encourage her, give her voice, and allow her to be everything she wants to be. Little girls who can dream do become women with vision when we all stand behind her.

What to Take Away?

Our girls are the future for all women. They are the reason we must succeed today. What can we learn and observe from these stories of women helping give girls voice?

#Reflect

You are never too young to start. Often we believe we must know more, have experienced more, and accomplished more before we make a start. In reality, your voice matters and you can make a difference big or small at any age. Everything begins with just one small step. When you use your voice, you share it with so many more.

#Remember

What is normal for us, may not be normal for someone else. I was horrified to learn that women and girls in the developing world did not have access to sanitary products. While this is a challenging example, let it be a reminder that what we take for granted might not be so for someone else. What you have, and what you know can be of great help. Believe it, and share it.

#Do

Let gratitude be your anchor. Compared to most women and girls around the world, we are rich beyond measure. Let's commit to taking what we have and doing something with it. A mentor and dear friend of mine, Athena Katsaros, likes to call this "joyful responsibility," whereby with all our privilege, we have an obligation to take action, and do it from a place of joy, not guilt. We have access to almost everything we can imagine, so let's grasp our opportunities with both hands, and dish them out to others when we can.

CHAPTER 6

WHEN WE ALL HOLD THE TORCH

I may have lit the torch,
but you will carry the flame.

—ANONYMOUS

For most armed service people, being deployed overseas is a mix of emotions. Some of these emotions include pride to serve one's country, excitement for an opportunity to put into practice everything you have trained for, and some trepidation, and likely fear of what is to come. So, imagine what that's like for an active-duty servicewoman, who is not only a mother but also a single mother. Joining the US Army as a single parent is not even possible, as Stewart Smith wrote for Balance Careers in 2019. It's one of the few restrictions to enlisting, along with your age, health, criminal record, and citizenship. But just like the stresses and strains of all relationships, not every marriage will make it. Cited in 2019 by Rod Powers from The Balance, a personal finance advisory, about 8 percent of all military members are single parents—11 percent of those for the Army, 8 percent for the Navy, 5 percent for the Air Force.

That's not the reason I was talking to Colonel Candice E. Frost, who was an active-duty single mom of two for half a decade in the US Army. But it comes up in my conversation with her, and is yet another reason to be inspired and surprised by her decorated military career. Now in her early forties, Candice is not only a glass-ceiling-breaker extraordinaire in the US Army, she is a powerful advocate for women's advancement and their access to opportunity across the military. Candice is currently director for the Army G-2 within the Headquarters, Department of the Army. The biography on her website explains she assesses foreign technical threats and provides intelligence assessments in support of Army acquisition programs, science and technology efforts, and research and development programs. She leads and supervises an organization of sixty-two personnel.

I got to know Candice in mid-2020; we had both been winners of the Business Council of Peace, Women Forward Awards, being honored for our commitment and contribution to advancing women in the workplace. She had given a raising speech that blew us all away, sharing her tenacity, belief, and steadfast actions in bringing other women forward through opportunity creation in the military. A lifelong champion for mentoring and leadership development, Candice had broken just about every glass ceiling she could muster within the US Army, and she had prepared a path to ensure that women could lead and serve in all roles in the military. I was curious about what led her to take these pioneering steps and what we could learn from her actions to help empower other women. I reckoned if Candice could do this for women in the military with all its traditions and centuries old male dominated roles, then there was something we could all surely do in civilian life to help a sister thrive.

WHERE IT ALL BEGAN FOR CANDICE

Candice grew up in Muscatine, Iowa, a small Midwest town along the Mississippi River. Smart academically and a great cross-country runner, at college age, she had been recruited for several universities to run for them. A high school career guidance counselor had first suggested West Point as a college option for her. Candice recalls being told, "you know, we've never had a woman go to a service academy from our school, and it could be perfect for you." She thought the idea was crazy. Neither of her parents had served in the military, and, by her own admission, they were "very, very, very liberal." It had not been in any kind of consideration to join a military academy, but she was curious, and on hearing it was a "free" ivy league education, she applied, not telling anyone but her parents.

Laughing, Candice recounts, "Lo and behold I was at a Bob Dylan concert when I got accepted to West Point. That tells you the kind of the music I listened to, and how much getting into the army was a huge eye opener for me." She had mused that her upbringing and liberal outlook on life might have made her unsuitable for a military career.

That wasn't the case though, Candice joined West Point in 1994 and thrived. She fell in love with soldiering. At the start, she did not know a thing about the defense department or national security, but she told me she knew how to push herself to be better and challenge herself physically, morally, emotionally, and mentally. Those were exceptional skills for budding young recruits. However, it was also at the US Military Academy that she experienced her first inequity.

Candice explained, "I grew up believing I could be anything I wanted to be, now I was in a world where roles are filtered by your gender alone. I kept buttressing up against that, it wasn't an environment I was used to." She confessed that there were multiple times at West Point where she could have stepped out and walked away, but she never did. "I think if you really believe in something, then you have to show up. Often you have to be in the system to change the system," she remarked. People from the outside could assist and agitate, but in her mind, if you are in the system, you can do more to open doors and create lasting change.

At West Point, Candice developed and established one of the first programs to prevent sexual assault and harassment at the academy. What started as an informal mentoring group focused on studies and physical training, quickly became the organization for women dealing with abuse at the academy. She won the respect of staff and faculty and, with their support, became the sounding board for new initiatives to support women.

She cared deeply for the military—its values, its people, and purpose—and she saw great possibilities for opening up opportunities for women to contribute to the betterment of the entire organization. Candice admitted it had not been one single event that had led her to drive herself harder to succeed in this male-dominated profession. It had been an accumulation of experiences and learning, which for more than a decade, led her to personally challenge the Army's conventional ways and mentor other women forward in the pursuit of adding more females to the ranks.

There were some highlights that had pushed Candice onward, as reported by The Cycle Staff at MSNBC in February 2013, like being chosen as the first woman to join the infantry brigade in the 82nd Airborne Division. That's the elite division of the US Army, specializing in parachute assault operations into denied areas and required to "respond to crisis contingencies anywhere in the world within eighteen hours." She was the only woman out of about 5,500 men, jumping out of airplanes and still carrying the same amount of gear. Getting this honor came with its drawbacks. A vocal minority of her colleagues definitely made it clear how they felt about her accomplishments.

"Some people definitely let it be known I was not welcome, even retired previous division commanders let me know that."

—CANDICE FROST

THE IMPORTANCE OF CHAMPIONS AND SUPPORTERS

What stood out to me while speaking with Candice about her equally demanding and inspiring stories was her upbeat attitude. She told me how she could have spent the time wallowing and feeling sorry for herself from the occasional backblast of verbal abuse she received in the 82 Airborne, but instead she pushed on, looking out to the horizon for the bright lights and the helpers.

One such helper had been her sergeant major, who affectionately called her Smurfette, but was in fact a gnarly US Army veteran who would run two miles while simultaneously smoking a cigarette. He was an educator and wanted her to succeed. She told me he would say, "Get over here, let me teach you these things."

In Candice's view, it had certainly been her own tenacity, attitude, and ability to rise above that got her started, but it was the handful of allies cheering her on, saying "Hey, I want you to make a difference, I want you to do this," that kept her going. She surrounded herself only with those who were willing to listen and help. She had been lucky to have a core group of people support her, but she wanted that for all women soldiers as a minimum. Placing women in the highest office in the US Army was her ultimate goal.

Candice began planning how to train the next generation of women leaders after attending the School of Advance Military studies in 2009, and being only one of two women of the 108 soldiers. Already limited in active combat roles, women who couldn't gain access to elite training had potential advancement opportunities further reduced. As she rose in seniority, she took every chance to bring the women in her sphere along with her. She became a vocal proponent in particular of women joining the Army's elite leadership program—Ranger School—and even went so far to call out the facilities during a building remodel, constantly challenging them to make sure they installed a women's restroom. "When I worked in an infantry brigade with only men, there was only one bathroom. So how do you make change if you don't even recognize the potential to have women?" She took every chance possible to raise awareness of equal opportunity for women in the armed forces.

Her persistence paid off. The US had long trained military officers from partner nations, but the US military barred all women from training for infantry, armor, and Special Forces occupations and from attending Ranger School. That all changed in 2016 when all positions in the Army were opened to women, explained Ellen Haring for the *Army Times* in 2020. While Candice wasn't able to join Ranger School herself, as Battalion Commander, she immediately started preparing her female soldiers to enroll. Her Brigade Commander questioned why she had been so "hell-bent" on getting women into Ranger School. In the 2020 book *Women Forward* from Toni Maloney and Joan Harper, Candice is quoted as saying "in the Army we wear symbols on our uniforms which speak much louder than words. A Ranger's tab means you're in the club. I wanted women in the club."

Candice cheered on the first graduates in 2016. She was not surprised that as of April 2020, the *Army Times* continued to report that of the fifty female graduates, "notably, not a single woman has ever been dropped from Ranger School for lack of motivation or quitting, as happens with men in every class." Perhaps the tattoo from Captain Emily Lilly, the oldest woman—at thirty-nine—and the first National Guard woman to graduate from Ranger School in 2018, sums up women's attitudes in the military, "The question is not who will let me, but who will stop me." After talking with Candice, I was convinced that's her motto too. Her quest did not end there though. She developed an Emerging Leader program designed to provide mentoring and physical readiness training to both men and women applying to Ranger School.

In the book *Women Forward*, she talks about her first deployment as Company Commander in Afghanistan in 2004-2005. Candice demanded that women were not housed separately, but allowed to live alongside the male troops in their unit. This change served as the example used to challenge direct combat laws and demonstrated that women were ready to lead in positions throughout the Army. "I believe the real work of leading and building a cohesive team is done before you get to the battlefield. Every one of my 127 soldiers had to trust me and my decisions," said Candice. How would that have been possible if their female commander lived in separate quarters? I'm struck by how groundbreaking that must have been, as it wasn't until January 2013 that Pentagon Chief, Leon Panetta, lifted a ban that prohibited women from serving in combat by opening up thousands of frontline positions.

As of 2019, the Army has successfully transferred more than one thousand women into the previously closed occupations of infantry, armor, and field artillery, according to the website

Military.com. By comparison, in numbers obtained by *Army Times* in the same year, the service had 19,820 junior enlisted infantrymen alone. It's clear there's a long way to go, but the fact women have expanded their footprint in combat arms and are taking command of units that have been exclusively male for centuries is a lot of progress in the five short years since that Defense Department ruling opened all military jobs to all troops.

Specifically talking to Candice about her time serving on the front lines got me curious as to whether women fight differently from men. I felt myself asking her the question and regretting it immediately. It seemed like a crude, naive gendered question. Candice didn't blink, "I don't think women fight differently, but we may bring a diverse idea or thought or unique method to apply something from training to actual fighting, and that benefits everyone. If in the world everything looks like a nail, and all you have is a hammer, that's what you use. So what if instead I have a multi-tool like a Swiss Army knife? I want the best players on my team. That's what I really love about bringing forward a new generation of woman soldiers, we are bringing additional perspectives, and additional skills to succeed together." Amen to that.

ONE OF THE HARDEST TIMES SHE EXPERIENCED

It hadn't always been easy for Candice, not only enduring the typical sexism you might imagine, but she was physically assaulted while on active duty for "Operation Enduring Freedom" in Afghanistan. She recounted, "I think it was one of the hardest times I had in service." At the time, she was a major and senior to an Australian officer who she had called out for his lack of diligence. It's worth noting that Candice is known for being straightforward and candid (her website and blog is "Colonel Candid"). The multinational partner officer took great offense at being called out in public and reacted violently, punching her in the chest. Candice was stunned it had happened, and she was stunned even more when her French Legionnaire boss ordered her to walk up to her assaulter and apologize to him for what she had done.

"I was aghast," Candice recounted. "I said to him, if your daughter had just been assaulted, would you tell her to walk up to the person who hit her and apologize?"

He retorted, of course he wouldn't do that. She reminded him that it was exactly what he had told her to do moments earlier. She asked him if they could please rethink his order. Further explaining, she was planning on pressing charges and her write up of events would include this conversation in which she said, "I would like to have you on my side, and be on my team rather than have to explain why you want me to apologize to someone who just assaulted me."

It has been an eye-opening event, but also a critical lesson of the importance and courage to advocate for yourself regardless of the situation. Back at her American command, General Lennington was incensed after hearing of the matter and became her biggest advocate. "It doesn't happen to American officers. It doesn't happen to American people," Candice recalled him saying. They never said American female, they said this does not happen to American officers. It had meant a lot to Candice to know they were on her side.

Today, women are still a minority in the US Army and especially in combat arms. Women make up just 14 percent of the Army's enlisted and 19 percent of its officer corps, according to 2018 data from the Council on Foreign Relations, a US foreign policy think tank. Candice bemoans there are still too many voices out there that women hear every day saying you can't do it. But the numbers are changing and the actions of Candice and others are part of the collective effort to bring women in the Army forward. She excitedly proclaims, "I want to be the person on the mountaintop that shouts, 'you can do this!' I want to be that voice to advocate and elevate women, and for men to shout the same thing. Let's make our army the best that it can be and take care of all of our people." One of her mantras is to become a role model and to have the gravitas to rally other women around you. I reckon she nailed it.

Cutting a path that doesn't exist, doing everything you can to keep going, having to fight so hard makes bringing others forward in your wake seem like the only natural and right thing to do. In my career, when I finally refound the voice of my youth, I too wanted to use it to advocate for other women. Candice and I had to create those opportunities for ourselves, just like countless other women, but it shouldn't have been that hard.

Candice has been a torchbearer in the US Army, shining a light on women across all ranks for the past twenty years, while illuminating a path for others to follow. Her work in mentoring, building advancement programs, educating her male colleagues, and calling out what's lost when women cannot lead, are manifesting and magnifying a fire that more beacons will be lit. Because of Candice and others like her, now more women can see themselves both serving and making it to the highest levels of leadership. It makes me wonder how women in these higher ranks over time might change the entire profession and how it works at its core. What might happen when we not only pass the light to the next woman, but when we all can hold the torch?

What to Take Away?

In a world where the military is one of the most male dominated places in the world, Candice was able to still make a real difference. It's a true testament that change is possible even in the most rigid of systems. While Candice had often been the first throughout her military career, she has made sure she will not be the last. As empowered women, it's something we can all strive to do.

#Remember

Change happens at the source; you are exactly where you need to be. Laws need to be changed and new policies adopted, but systemic change must happen everywhere. You know your organization's challenges and opportunities for women better than anyone. You likely know who and how to get a shift to happen. Rocking the boat might be risky, but lasting sea changes cannot be made without a call to chart a new course. You can be an advocate for change no matter where you are.

#Reflect

Challenging authority in the military could have been mutinous, but Candice acted in a clever and respectful way within an organization she loved. She wanted to make the US Army better, not only for herself and other women, but as a whole with women fully contributing. You can challenge your organization respectfully and make a difference, and it's for the good of everyone.

#Do

One of Candice's mantras is to become a role model. That all starts with you working on yourself first. When empowering other women, we can often forget how we show up is just as important as what we do and say in terms of signaling to others what is possible. So whatever your role and position, be the best at what your job is today. You are not only advancing yourself and your impact, but you are also demonstrating success is achievable.

CHAPTER 7

IT TAKES A VILLAGE

———

Here's to strong women. May we know them.
May we be them. May we raise them.

—UNKNOWN

In 2012, Anne-Marie Slaughter wrote a now-infamous cover article for *The Atlantic* entitled, "Why Women Still Can't Have It All." As her biography on New America in 2021 describes, she was the first woman to serve as the director of policy planning for the US State Department. She had chosen not to renew her tenure working for then US Secretary of State Hillary Clinton, and instead return home to be with her family and focus on her teaching career at Princeton. The nature of her deeply personal and high-profile story finally publicly named what all women already knew—the mistaken belief that we could raise a family and have a career in equal measure.

At the time *The Atlantic* piece came out, I was working at Mozilla, and it had been "the" topic of conversation, stirring up many emotions. My female colleagues, some who were first-time moms, were equally struggling to commute two hours per day in Bay Area traffic, hold down a demanding full-time job, run a household, and also be the mom they wanted to be.

HAVING IT ALL

I had seen it for myself, growing up in a small town in the UK. My mum was an in-betweener. She felt she couldn't work full time so she could be there for me, but she still wanted to work. In the early years, she had to work to keep food on the table and me in new school shoes. Mum was a part-time milliner following in my grandmother's footsteps, who in her own retirement took care of me every afternoon after school and during the school holidays. My mum felt there was no way she could have a career, but on the other hand, with her part-time job, she couldn't be a full-time mum either.

This view that women could have everything they wanted if they simply endured the pain of striving and sacrifice had persisted for decades. It was largely attributed to Helen Gurley Brown, editor-in-chief of *Cosmopolitan* magazine for thirty-two years, who wrote the book *Having It All* in 1982. As Marie-Claire Chappet wrote for *Glamour* magazine in 2019, it documented Gurley Brown's advice for career success and having everything you want as a woman. Yet, ironically, she had no children herself.

Anne-Marie Slaughter had left Washington and returned to Princeton as a professor. This lifestyle allowed her to set her own schedule, rather than the rigidity of an office job in Washington. In *The Atlantic* article, she admitted she was speaking on behalf of her own demographic, "highly educated, well-off women who are privileged enough to have choices in the first place." According to Sophia Kerby at the policy institute, Centre for American Progress in 2012, that's clearly not the case for millions of other women with no choice, who are more often than not single mothers and women of color just trying to make ends meet.

In recent years, the world has made little progress to become more mother friendly. Over the past ten years, Dr Bryan Robinson for *Forbes* reports "over fifty thousand pregnancy discrimination claims were filed with the Equal Employment Opportunity Commission and Fair Employment Practices Agencies in the United States." Discrimination included everything from hiring, firing, pay, job assignments, promotions, layoff, training, and fringe benefits such as leave and health insurance. In one *Science Magazine* study cited by Lesley Evans Ogden in 2019, "women who didn't have children were two times more likely to be called for an interview, as compared with similarly qualified mothers." Another study from the same year, referenced by Jessica Dickler at CNBC, "showed that for women, incomes drop 30 percent after giving birth for the first time and they never catch up."

Sheryl Sandberg, author of the cultural phenomena book *Lean In,* tried to take a unique approach to the same subject of having it all. Her book's message, as described by Caitlin Gibson in *The Washington Post* in 2018, is "If a woman works hard enough, and asserts herself enough, she can thrive at home *and* at work." It had been a huge success.

The article reports it ranked on *The New York Times* bestseller list for more than a year and sold over four million copies. However, it also received mixed reviews almost as soon as it was released in 2013, which focused on Sheryl's unique position and privilege of being the number two C-Level executive at Facebook—one of the largest companies on the planet with all its advantages.

Over the years, Sheryl Sandberg herself has had to acknowledge that her efforts in creating the "Lean In" social movement had not translated to increased numbers of women in leadership. In 2021 Alyssa Newcomb for NBC News reported only 8.2 percent of Fortune 500 CEOs and 2 percent of S&P 500 CEOs are women. And those numbers are declining globally. In a 2017 *USA Today* interview with Jessica Guynn, Sheryl said, "in terms of women in leadership roles, we are not better off. [...] overall, we are not seeing a major increase in female leadership in any industry or in any government in the world, and I think that's a shame." Where *Lean In* was successful was the creation of "Lean In Circles," which is where small groups of professional women come together to support one another. That had taken off like a rocket ship and is still as popular today with their website claiming more than fifty thousand circles have been created in 184 countries. The idea to make it easier for women to help other women was a key part of the success.

IT TAKES A VILLAGE

It was her female network that had helped my friend, Erika Murdock Balbuena, take her dream role as Global Head of

Impact Computing at Amazon Web Services. She was four and a half months pregnant when she started the role. She had to commute to Seattle from the Bay Area to work every week, which she did for three months right up until her second daughter was born. Erika explained to me that with a job offer on the table, she had agonized over her decision, "I only knew of fathers doing this. I didn't have any examples of women in my life doing this."

So she used her network, the one she'd worked hard to build over the past few years. She bravely explained how a number of women in her life had told her to "go for it." Yes, it would be hard on her and her husband, but her newborn and toddler would not remember these early years of their lives when she was away, so do it now and be there in the coming years when her daughters were older would need her more.

Erika also told me she couldn't have made this big career decision without her husband. She reminded me that Sheryl Sandberg had been right about one thing when she said the most important career choice you'll make is who you choose as your partner. She wrote in her book *Lean In*, "I don't know of one woman in a leadership position whose life partner is not fully—and I mean fully—supportive of her career." Erika's husband had been a massive supporter of her taking this big step and had "frankly picked up the home slack way more than I did," she explained. Erika wisely went on to share, "The more you're married, the more you will come up against these big life moments that cause you to evaluate short-term challenge for long-term gain. It's important to have a supportive, equal partnership because we don't do this alone."

What I love about Erika's story and her attitude was that she was completely conscious of the choices she was making. She explained to me, "I don't even like the phrase 'have it all' because no one person on this Earth has it all. It's not even a balancing act. To me, it's a dance."

"Sometimes you pick up a dance partner, that's career advancement. Sometimes you pick up a partner, that's family, sometimes you pick up a partner, that's money, but you can't dance with everyone at the same time."

—ERIKA MURDOCK BALBUENA

Erika sagely shared that when you make a decision that impacts your home life in this big of a way, one must choose the things driving our decision, commit to them, and then work toward those goals. It was all possible because she had family and resources to help, a husband who had her back, and a strong network of friends and women to help her make the right choice for her.

THE WORLD NEEDS MOTHERS!

Regardless of what women are enduring and going through, the support of other women can be a game changer. This knowledge is what led Katya Libin to cofound HeyMama—the quickly growing social network for working moms. It was a thrill for me to interview Katya. She started her company from a personal pain point when she had her daughter. She was in her twenties and living in New York City. The only moments she could interact with other women was on the playground and at school meetings.

She craved connection with other working moms, "I didn't have many places to get advice on how to navigate my career and motherhood, and do so with as much sanity and grace as possible." She began imagining a concept around HeyMama, where ambitious, passionate, and creative business-women and mothers from around the world could grow and learn together. As reported by Jordan Crook at *TechCrunch* in 2020, the young company raised several million dollars in seed investment funding, including from fashion brand icon Rebecca Minkoff. Not bad for what had been a severely over-looked demographic.

Talking of good business sense, Katja told me she had spoken many times about the "motherhood advantage," which is where women take skills they gained from motherhood and adapt them to their roles. She explained that becoming a mother re-triggers parts of your brain and expands lots of different valuable emotional skills that translate exceptionally well into the workplace. "Empathy, compassion, communication, patience, negotiation, I mean, who hasn't negotiated with their toddler, and kept their head on straight?"

These are all the skills that are needed in the corporate world right now during the COVID-19 pandemic. Data revealed in 2020 by Shelcy V. Joseph for *Forbes*, stated 49 percent of hiring managers valued the strong work ethic of working moms, plus their time management skills and patience. I heard her little one screaming in the background and thought, oh yes—folks have no idea how much strength, patience, and tenacity women have.

Evidence further shared by Jack Zenger and Joseph Folkman in 2019 for the *Harvard Business Review* shows that "women score higher than men in most leadership skills such as taking initiative, acting with resilience, practicing self-development, driving for results, and displaying high integrity and honesty." In fact, they were thought to be more effective in 84 percent of the competencies most frequently measured. What's holding women back is not lack of capability, but unconscious bias and, therefore, a dearth of opportunity.

Earlier this year, HeyMama went a step further and launched Motherhood on the Resume (MOTR), encouraging women to add "mother" to their resume. The campaign aims to validate the unpaid labor of moms, destigmatize taking time off from work for motherhood, and recognize the strengths moms bring to their professional lives, not in spite of being parents but because of it.

Katya walked me through stories of how her community of entrepreneur and corporate moms are supporting each other. "It's so unifying, because you know what the other women have been through. And it gives you a whole new sense of hope." Her community had come too late for some. Katya shared a heartbreaking conversation she had with a Fortune 500 woman leader only the week before. She had confided with Katya that there were women at her company who had to sacrifice so much, "they had chosen not to have children and deeply regretted it, there simply wasn't a path for them to have kids, and a successful career."

Today, Katya is witnessing promising shifts happening within the corporate landscape, with motherhood taking a much bigger role in equity, inclusion, and parenting overall. It's good news. Mothers are expecting more from their employers, and employers are realizing that if they don't provide support and opportunity, they will be at risk for these women leaving, which comes at a huge cost to companies. Katya shared that HeyMama has been breaking ground by "providing group memberships to companies to help them invest in their talent, and drive engagement and loyalty to moms, in a way that I don't think would have been top of mind many years ago."

One of HeyMama's biggest supporters is the Lincoln Motor Company. For several years, they have chosen to invest in the success of their working mothers, according to the 2021 HeyMama website. Katya was right when she said that at a first glance you wouldn't necessarily think a car company is going to be the one to show up for working mothers, but this company has done exactly that. "They have been a phenomenal partner on all levels, expanding our mentorship program and showing it's not about the industry or what your company does, but about your commitment to this demographic of women who need tools and resources behind them."

In 2020, Joy Falotico, president at Lincoln, and Serena Williams, a brand ambassador for the company, came together for the HeyMama Summit. They discussed their role as successful women thriving in male-dominated spaces. Joy said there is still a long way to go before women achieve true equity. "The first thing we need is flexibility in work policies, and parental leave policies that engage mothers back into the workforce... women also need equity—in pay, in opportunity, and the resources to be successful because of all the things that we're balancing."

That has never been truer, as the COVID-19 pandemic has upended work and home life. As reported by Ina Fried for Axios in 2020, even with companies like Salesforce, PepsiCo, Uber, and Pinterest recently signing a pledge to offer more flexibility and resources for working parents, women have carried an outsized share of the burden, and they are more likely to lose a job and more likely to shoulder the load of closed schools and day care.

According to the US Bureau of Labor Statistics, American women lost more than five million jobs in 2020 due to the pandemic, and Black women were among the most affected with over 154,000 Black women leaving the labor force in December 2020 alone. And, with 85 percent of Black mothers said to be the primary, sole, or co-breadwinner for their families, Black moms and Black families are struggling, which was reported by Sarah Jane Glynn for American Progress in 2019.

As with every chapter I have written—the weight and burden of the plight of women—our equity and progress is always apparent. There is always a part where I have struggled to explain all the challenges we face, especially as we mark over one year of the pandemic and the increased hardships it has brought women. I wonder if I spend too long bemoaning our strife, and if I have painted a picture that seems unsurmountable to solve. But then, with equal measure, I hope you find yourself moved and inspired by the women standing up, taking chances, and making choices that are 100 percent right for them. Women like Erika, who chose her career with her eyes wide open, a strong role model to other women, and even more so to her two young daughters. And, women like Katya creating spaces for working mothers to equally build their careers and their families together.

Full disclosure, I am not a mom and hesitated in writing about this subject because I didn't feel I had the personal experience to speak on behalf of mothers. I carried on though because over my working life, I have seen friends become moms and give up their careers. I have seen them agonize over whether they should have a second child. I've seen them leave their husbands to choose the path that's right for them. I have seen them struggle, lament, and sometimes envy my seemingly carefree existence sans kids. What I have learned is that while we desperately still need the systemic change to welcome, support, and allow working mothers to thrive, it is a community of women empowering women who will keep us going, and help us raise a strong, bold, and passionate next generation. "The world needs mothers!" Katya had exclaimed in our interview—I wholeheartedly agree!

What to Take Away?

We can't have it all, that was always clear, but if we allow ourselves to be in full awareness of our options and in full choice of our decisions, more can be available to us. Life is made up of polarities, none more so than in career versus family. With such complicated and important topics, we need a powerful community around us to help us see all the possibilities, and to help us find the best path forward with ease, grace, and joy.

#Do

Erika explained wisely that you cannot dance with more than one partner at a time. I love the idea of sharing this metaphor with other women in your life who are trying to make it all work. Help her define what's most important in this moment, so she might have focus and commitment. But also help her see that when she makes a choice, it is not a zero-sum game. It does not have to be at the expense of something else entirely, rather our other important priorities must be integrated in new ways.

#Do

Offer your perspective, not your advice. Letting a working mom choose the path that is right for her is ever more important. These decisions may be some of the biggest of her life, and so it's key that she has impartial and nonjudgmental people in her camp. Always start questions with "what" rather than "how." (What would that look like? What would that give you? What else is possible?) An open conversation will allow her to process all her thoughts, fears, and opportunities.

#Remember

Don't forget to help moms and soon-to-be moms to see the possibilities. Tune your ears to self-defeating talk and playing small. Allow the women in your life to make the decisions that are right for her and her family, but do not neglect to help her see what else might be true. We should never be afraid of calling out all the options and then allowing her to make a final choice. Not seeing the full picture could be a missed opportunity.

CHAPTER 8

LEADING BY EXAMPLE

The most difficult thing is the decision
to act, the rest is merely tenacity.

—AMELIA EARHART

For many years I have called Mitchell Baker the "Mother of the Internet." It's a title she isn't wholly keen on, but she doesn't deny it, and she doesn't fight me on it either. Mitchell is the cofounder of Mozilla, the organization behind the Firefox web browser, and one of the biggest advocates for user privacy and a free and open internet. As one of the few women leaders in technology, and especially so since the early days of the internet, she is a widely celebrated and closely watched figure. Marc Andreessen, in *Time* magazine, called Mitchell one of the most influential people in the world in 2005, and I'm proud to say she has been my role model for more than a decade.

I had the great honor of working directly for Mitchell as her chief of staff from 2015 to 2018. Before that, I worked alongside her at Mozilla for half a decade more. Mitchell is a character; I know she won't mind my saying that. She is quirky in both her mannerisms and fashion choices. Speaking technology, legalese, strategy, and Mandarin, she commands respect across the spectrum. One of her many skills is being razor smart at understanding and distilling complexity. Mitchell is a true visionary. Oh, and she is a trapeze artist flying the high wire!

Mitchell is also a massive voice for women's empowerment. Dedicated to advancing women in technology by championing programs such as Outreachy—an internship program that supports diversity in free and open source software— or TechWomen—an initiative launched by the US Department of State to bring forward women leaders in science, technology, engineering, and mathematics (STEM) across Africa, Central and South Asia, and the Middle East. She also served on the UN High Level Panel for Women's Economic Empowerment. Mitchell cares deeply that women be active participants and leaders in digital life and, as she explains on her blog in 2016, profoundly believes the internet can play a key role in improving the lives and opportunities of women and girls.

ACTIVE ROLE MODELS ARE CRUCIAL

It hadn't always been that way. In my early days, around 2007 when Firefox was exploding and I headed up marketing for Mozilla in Europe, Mitchell had shied away from journalist's personal questions about her role as one of so few women leaders in technology. On press tour together in Germany and London, I would see her fend off questions about her family and how she coped with it all. And then there were the endless questions about her hair. Almost every reporter wanted to bring it up. She is known for her iconic asymmetric hairstyle: shaved on one side, curled around her face on the other, and colored bright red. It was usually the case to hear folks say it resembled the Firefox logo. More than once, I remember Mitchell would be less than amused at their overtly gendered, bordering on rude questions, and I could see a flash go across her face that she was contemplating walking out.

That had all changed five or six years ago when she realized her status as this self-called "oddball woman in tech," a woman who had made it in technology, and had a big voice and influence was not enough to help bring forward more women leaders behind her. She told me, "I assumed the role model piece alone was enough, but after a while I saw it wasn't, and I needed to be more intentional about change." From the moment I met Mitchell, I was drawn to her unique style of leadership, and she became one of my first female role models. However, out in the world it was clear Mitchell could take on a more highly active and visible role, which could go a long way to creating systemic change for women in technology.

One day, early in the Firefox phenomena, her husband Casey had pinned a local Bay Area newspaper two-page feature about her to her son's grade school classroom message board. Recoiling as she remembered the moment, Mitchell shared, "I was appalled! You know my son's friends and their parents are going to come to school see these pictures of me on the noticeboard!" It all seemed like showing off. Casey had said to her, "look if you want both girls and boys to have different role models, you will have to show them. I was still a little bit appalled. But I decided he was right. So that was personally a pretty big turning point."

Mitchell shared, "Even in my own organization where I was the cofounder, it wasn't enough." It was during a difficult time at Mozilla when she could finally see the implicit bias surrounding her. "I was listening to a set of the men around me who had worked with and for me for quite some time, and I heard the comments they were making about women in front of me, and I thought to myself just being here is not enough—this is not acceptable," Mitchell explained. She set out to deliberately find ways to support more women. She would pull people into conversations, learning more about what they were experiencing before thoughtfully considering a set of actions that could help.

USING HER VOICE AND INFLUENCE

In 2015, Mitchell first began by answering the calls for funding women's program initiatives within Mozilla. I remember distinctly Lukas Blakk, advisory board member at the Ada Initiative—a nonprofit focused on increasing participation of women in open technology—and also Mozilla's release manager for Firefox, asking if it was in the budget to send Mozilla women to the annual Grace Hopper conference. Mitchell said yes, and this became an annual event inside Mozilla for female computer scientist employees to attend the largest gathering event for women in computing. I never attended, but I was delighted for my colleagues who were thrilled to go. They always came back with inspiring stories and learning from the sessions designed to bring women in computing forward.

Even though Mitchell never encountered direct resistance within Mozilla toward these kinds of programs advancing women, she would often hear that "this might not be the right time, or it's going to take us longer to have a full program," or you know, "this really isn't gonna work," she told me.

"I had to put my foot down and say 'no, we're starting now.' Maybe it's not fully formed or perfect, but we're not going to wait any longer."

—MITCHELL BAKER

Mitchell went on to steadily fund and dedicate more time to diversity and inclusion work. Eventually it became pervasive enough for it to become a core focus of then CEO Chris Beard, and therefore the whole organization as documented publicly in 2018 on the Mozilla blog.

From my own experiences in my past years as chief of staff, I saw Mozilla work hard to add women into leadership roles, make sure women joined the Mozilla board of directors, and externally, more women at Mozilla were mentors and role models for women in technology. I saw the direct and intentional influence Mitchell had within the organization to create change, and be both the reminder and bottom line for an inclusive culture where all people could thrive.

After almost a year of enduring the Bay Area COVID-19 lockdown, I asked Mitchell in our interview, what she was most hopeful about moving forward. She took a moment to think. Mitchell is known for her long pauses as she constructs an always thoughtful reply. Over the years of working together, I had always put this down to her legal training and her early career as a top lawyer at Netscape. After our intimate conversation, now I think perhaps it's a habit that was left over from her being the "only" woman in the room for the longest time, and she had to be careful what she said.

She responded by saying, "I'm hopeful we can build a world where it feels natural to actually look at and want different perspectives, different people, and different ideas. Where that is seen as positive and normal." I've heard this many times before from Mitchell. It's a fundamental belief of how Mozilla believes the internet should be built and organized. The Mozilla mission was always to build the internet as a global public resource that must remain open and accessible." I told Mitchell I was smiling as I recalled the last big project she and I did together and how crucially important it is to bring all voices to the table.

We developed and launched all transparently in the public domain the key operating principles that form the foundation for Mozilla's work, which were then added as an addendum to the Mozilla Manifesto. They include principles such as being committed to an "internet that catalyzes collaboration among diverse communities working together for the common good." In terms of working on the key project with Mitchell, I had said at the time it was my life's work. Now several years on, I still feel a deep sense of pride and resonance of our work that shaped Mozilla and my own beliefs on how the world ought to be. I created The Coaching Fellowship with the core principle of creating access for young women social change leaders and bringing them together in service of building a more equitable world.

Mitchell is quirky to the end. I reminded her she was one of only two other women inducted into the inaugural class of the Internet Hall of Fame, along with Vinf Serf, Tim Bernes Lee, and Al Gore. For a moment she questioned if that was true and did a quick internet search to check. Yes, it was true and we digressed for a moment to talk about the "Klingon dress" she wore, the name christened by her husband. It's a fabulous long black and gold spacey number. She looked as striking as ever. In many ways, it's a typical thing for Mitchell not to recall the many awards and honors bestowed upon her. In all the years I've known her, it was always about the impact she could make, but never about her. Though, as Anne Kramer wrote for Protocol in January 2021, where I was featured, the cult of her leadership runs deep with every Mozillian whether past or present, we all still care enormously for her and the Mozilla mission.

Mitchell has been the Chief Lizard Wrangler at Mozilla for over twenty years, and in 2020 she took on the role of CEO (for the second time). Alas, she is still a rarity as a woman commanding such influence on our daily lives. In the early part of 2021, Alyssa Newcomb for NBC News reported only forty-one women led Fortune 500 companies. That equates to 8.2 percent, but believe it or not it's an improvement from the thirty-three companies in 2019 and twenty-four in 2018... going back twenty years, there were just two companies on the list that were run by women.

THE ROLE MODELS OF SILICON VALLEY

In the many years of knowing and working with Mitchell, she has always said to me that if you are a woman in a position of influence it's your responsibility, perhaps even your obligation to help encourage, mentor, champion, and provide opportunities for more women to rise. She is in good company, one other rare and influential female leader in the technology industry, who also believes this at her core is Obi Felten, Head of Getting Moonshots Ready for the Real World at X, Alphabet's moonshot factory. You met Obi in Chapter 2 when she explained the importance of a strong female network to succeed.

An extended 2018 *Financial Times* article by Hannah Kuchler said, we have Obi to thank "there are self-driving cars on the streets, internet-beaming balloons in the sky and burritos delivered by drones." Her unique talent is understanding the edge of new technologies and bringing them to the real world. She is also a loud and action-focused advocate for diversity and inclusion.

When Obi arrived in Silicon Valley, she immediately began noticing the dearth of women holding key technology or leadership roles—like my own experience of landing in "the Valley." This inspired her to become an active, rather than a latent, feminist. "I sought out other women because I realized quickly that was a shortcut to finding the really talented people," she went on to say in the FT interview. I've known Obi for several years now and have seen her inclusive and innovative work in the world blossom.

In my interview with Obi, I asked how it had all started. She recounted, she went straight to the top, and approached Astro Teller, the CEO of X, and said to him, "We care about diversity, but we need to do more to make faster progress. He asked me if I was volunteering, and I said yes, I suppose I am. But ,I can't do this on my own—we need a dedicated lead." Obi hired Gina Amaro Ruden as her Cultural Alchemist. A fantastic "black Puerto Rican from NYC" she told me, and together they got started. They planned to treat their diversity project, just like any other experimental project at X—where they would try new things, push the boundaries, take risks, learn, and iterate.

Obi and Gina began their experiment by focusing on the women who were already at X "because there was already a strong grassroots effort, a thriving employee resource group called Women of X," she explained. Gina had designed a leadership program for twelve women called "Thrive," which gave them access to intensive coaching for a year. They got buy-in from managers to let their people participate by asking them to nominate potential candidates, so they had a stake in the process. That in itself had been an interesting learning for everyone involved, as when Obi asked the managers to nominate people, some had realized they had no women at all at that level to recommend. By raising awareness of diversity and inclusion, and increasing the leadership capabilities, X grew the number of women in leadership roles, as well as women overall. Obi said, "You can do it, if you really put your mind to it and if you've got strong grassroots efforts and support from the top."

Obi believes that unless we have the best talent at the table, we're not going to get the best outcomes. For her, it's about having people who ask different and better questions. For instance, she told a story about the early days of Wing, described on X website as, "an autonomous delivery drone service aiming to increase access to goods, reduce traffic congestion in cities, and help ease the CO_2 emissions attributable to the transportation of goods." The first idea was to deliver defibrillators to heart attack victims. Obi described, "Our research team tested this in the lab. They gave innocent bystanders a defibrillator and said, save this person's life. They found it took people six minutes to figure out how to use the defibrillator, so it was irrelevant that we delivered it in ninety seconds because after eight minutes the ambulance arrived anyway." The product was unlikely to save lives.

Based on these results, the researchers convinced the engineers to give up on the idea to deliver defibrillators. The researchers asked *why* we were delivering defibrillators and whether we were solving the right problem in the first place. They approached the problem completely differently to the rest of the team and changed the course of the project.

It turns out asking different questions could be a massive differentiator, as diversity is proven to boost innovation and financial results. In fact, more women in leadership, writes Caroline Castrillon at *Forbes* in 2019, has proven to increase employee satisfaction and engagement, and with more female executives in decision-making positions, companies generate stronger market returns and superior profits. Even Kevin O' Leary of *Shark Tank* fame admitted in an interview with Ali Montag for CNBC in 2018, that he prefers to invest in companies led by women because they produce superior returns. In Castrillon's article she shares, forty plus companies O' Leary invested in, 95 percent of those women-led companies met their financial targets, compared with just 65 percent for businesses with male leaders.

For Google X, they are focused on solving the world's biggest problems, and Obi thinks making our workplaces more inclusive can but only help by "bringing together the brightest, most diverse minds to work on creative solutions." She earnestly tells me, "Think about it. If you brought all this talent to the table that's currently neglected, not just in our society but in countries across the globe, you would have all that much more brain power to apply to these problems."

I think we are all singing from the same hymn sheet here. Just as Mitchell had said when all voices are heard and included, then great work can be done. Whether that's inside corporations making better products and increasing profits, or working on solving the biggest challenges in our lifetime. When the talents of women and diverse people are included, the possibilities, in my humble opinion, seem endless.

What to Take Away?

Endless possibilities are within reach, but only if we have more people in positions to be heard. If you are the one doing the listening, call upon different people for their advice and perspective. If you have influence, help ensure your people are hiring and developing women around you. If you run a project, ensure you have a diverse group of people to bring about the best innovative and creative solutions.

#Remember

Request more diverse perspectives. One tool Mitchell and I developed at Mozilla was the "MAP— Multiple Alternatives Perspectives" framework. A simple checklist of sorts to make sure we were including other voices in the decision-making process, be that from different departments, geographies, job levels, and, of course, diversity of gender and background. We used this framework in core hiring decisions and organization-wide projects. Seeking more voices can ensure you are not blind sighted, help get better outcomes, and build an inclusive culture by allowing more people to share their ideas, experience, and expertise.

#Do

Send the elevator down. That's where women who have made it to a significant position of power and influence support other women to also reach higher levels of leadership. I've heard this turn of phrase for years, and I have tried to implement it wherever

I could with promotions, salary raises, and hiring. We may not all be in a position to hire and move women and minorities into increased positions of responsibility. However, we still can be an ally and offer advice and support wherever we can to keep that person engaged, motivated, and ready for opportunities that come along.

#Do

Today, there are more people than ever before in positions of power, and they are listening to the needs of women and minorities in the workplace. Use this time to add your voice and lobby your manager and C-levels to increase their diversity, equity, and inclusion commitments, then hold them accountable for results and change. As we learned with Tracy Chou, encourage your organization to be publicly transparent about the diverse representation of leaders and report how they are doing every year. It is our responsibility if we have some power to help distribute it to others.

CHAPTER 9

THE VALUE OF INVESTING

———

Success isn't about how much money you make;
it's about the difference you make in people's lives.

— MICHELLE OBAMA

The adage "money makes the world go round" is as old as the hills. Money does indeed open doors, increase impact, and create change. It's a vehicle for success for every idea, passion, mission, company goal, and desire for change. The thing is money and women don't sit together really easily. It's complicated for lots of reasons.

The roots of the complex relationship between women and money begin with the way girls are not taught about money or even given good math skills in school, and this continues all the way through our lives. As recently as 2020, PayScale reported that women earned only eighty-one cents for every dollar earned by men. Many of us have trouble equating our worth with what we earn. We are shy when it comes to talking about money and advocating for our financial value. According to a 2021 report from staffing firm Randstad US, 60 percent of us have never negotiated about money with our employers. The dearth of female-friendly financial service products from savings accounts to retirement funds means we are often confused and intimidated by how to invest our money. You would think the cards are squarely stacked against us, but watch out world.

IT'S GOING TO CHANGE

A change is coming that will revolutionize the role women play in the financial world. According to McKinsey research in 2020 from Pooneh Baghai, Olivia Howard, Lakshmi Prakash, and Jill Zucker, "by 2030, American women are expected to control much of the $30 trillion in financial assets that baby boomers will possess—a potential wealth transfer of such magnitude that it approaches the annual GDP of the United States." As they say in their report, "after years of playing second fiddle to men, women are poised to take center stage."

Cat Berman, CEO of the impact investing platform CNote, had seen this day coming for years, and she is now part of the change. A few years back, I had hosted a "salon style" event in my living room when she was in the early stages of cofounding CNote. About a dozen of my friends and work colleagues of different ages and backgrounds gathered to share our experience with money and how we make financial decisions. The results shocked us all. Only a tiny number of us were investors (and then only dipping a single toe in the water). If we had any additional wealth, more than 90 percent of us put it into a savings account, including me. I was taught to be a good girl and save my pennies for a rainy day, but that was where the advice ended. We were all smart, accomplished, and successful women, and yet we had no clue how to make our hard-earned money work as hard for us as it did for our husbands and our male coworkers.

Our savings accounts were making close to zero interest while—according to James Royal, PhD and Arielle O'Shea for NerdWallet in May 2021—the average return on stock market investment was 10 percent. The missed earned revenue was not only a missed opportunity for today, but the compounded loss meant we were missing out on significant future wealth.

Three years later, Cat has built an award-winning company that was voted best new start-up at South by Southwest in 2017. She is the tip of the spear, creating change for investors and investees. It was great to sit down and talk with her again. I asked her what was really getting in the way of women investing their wealth.

"We are absolutely underserved when it comes to finances. We give too much prominence to safety and cash because of lack of information or not having a financial advisor. We also make less money, so at the end of the day, we don't have as much to invest," Cat exclaimed. In 2021, PayScale explained that over a forty-year period, women will have made $900,000 less than men, all of that compounding, so we have even less returns. Shockingly, that means women have to work one more year to retire from work.

"I mean, it's outrageous that the vast majority of financial advisors are still white men who head up family wealth advice and have never really taken the voice of women into account," Cat explained. "When I was at Charles Schwab, we found that when a spouse passes or when a woman divorces, over 70 percent of the time, the woman will fire her financial advisor because that financial advisor was only speaking to and taking direction from the husband. So when he was no longer in the picture, and it's the woman he has to talk to across that large mahogany desk, they both realize it's a bad fit."

Lastly, Cat points out that probably the most important reason women are underserved comes down to values. "We know over 75 percent of women will tell you they want to invest with their values." Women think about the world more holistically. We are not only thinking about a return on investment for one quarter, rather, we are thinking about what our investment will look like in the long-term. Equally as significant for women is, what is the impact of my investment in the world? What will the net effects be for my grandchildren? Women want to know the ethos of a company's CEO; they want to know how they do business and for the sake of what. They care about child labor, environmental impact, worker's rights, and a multitude of social issues.

The trouble is that so few products exist in terms of being able to invest with one's values and have the transparency of seeing where those investments are made. As women and other voices have not inherently been at the table, therefore, products have not been created to align with their values and requirements. Sally Krawcheck, founder and CEO at Ellevest, told Coryanne Hicks at US News in 2019, "Money in a capitalist society is power. So it shouldn't be surprising that the most capitalist industry is the most manly of industries."

Cat deeply understood what was really driving women's differentiated needs, their preferences, and behaviors. She built a company going much farther than helping women manage their money. "At CNote, we know that women are inheriting the majority of assets over the next two decades and we know that, if given the choice, women would rather invest in products that both give a great return and do good things for the world. Warren Buffett agrees that if you empower a woman, she ends up making a better investor."

However, that is only one half of the story. Cat built a company that not only provides a way to choose where you invest with full transparency, but it is also working toward solving the inherent issue that the vast majority of women entrepreneurs and underserved groups do not get access to funding. This is as true on Sandhill Road, the Mecca of Venture Capital in Silicon Valley, as it is in the local bank branches of small communities. In 2014, Cat was tired of the wealth gap and rising inequality, it was "just devastating, it felt like there was no hope in sight. I wrestled with the feeling of how each of us play a role in creating greater equality. It wasn't enough for me just to say, 'oh women should get more access to capital, and what can I do about that?' It was about addressing the systems that created these inequalities to begin with." That was when the page really turned for Cat.

Her goal for both her investors and entrepreneurs was wealth creation, prosperity for everybody. Any person, of any color, born in any place could get access to opportunity. There were few bright spots around the country on the front line of providing more economic justice to our communities, mainly in the form of community lenders (Community Development Financial Institution [CDFI] banks). CDFIs are private sector banks and credit unions. They loan funds that focus primarily on personal lending and business development efforts in low-income local communities that have historically been locked out of the financial system in the US. Yet, almost no American knew they existed. Cat exclaimed, "you know 99 percent of Americans had never even heard of a community lender?"

The challenge goes deeper. CDFI lenders were not well supported and funded themselves. A lack of fair capital and assistance was happening to the degree that it needed to because of those constraints. So that's when CNote decided to step in, innovating to make funding more accessible, supporting those CDFIs with funding, and figuring out how to institutionalize it so everybody could play a role in driving capital where it is needed most.

CNote's hard work over the years recently attracted the attention of the Mastercard Impact Fund. They made a $20 million investment into CDFIs through CNote's Promise Account product furthering CNote's support of women and minority-owned businesses in underserved communities across the US. I got the opportunity to speak with Marla Blow, the then-senior vice president, Social Impact,

North America at Mastercard's Center for Inclusive Growth, whose goal is to make the digital economy work for everyone everywhere.

> "I have to correct people all the time, stop saying that women are a minority, 50 percent of the population is not a minority!"

—MARLA BLOW

At the time Marla worked on securing the investment for CNote, she shared with me, "we are mobilizing to support and build up women-led businesses. Through our work with CNote, there is now a portfolio of up to twenty CDFIs that hold some of Mastercard's money on deposit and serve small rural communities and Black and Latinx led businesses. This is a great example of how large corporations can help drive the success, and foster the growth of woman-owned businesses."

Marla Blow is a bold and wicked smart, African American woman picked by Elizabeth Warren to work with her in building the first Consumer Financial Protection Bureau (CFPB) in the USA. Marla is also a successful entrepreneur who raised $40 million, which the *Washington Business Journal's* Andy Medici described in 2019, as "a rare haul for an African-American female founder, given that just 1 percent of black women founders end up getting venture backing of any kind." Marla used the funding to expand her company

FS Card Inc., a credit card designed to move small dollar loan customers into more traditional credit products, and she sold the business five years later. Marla is a powerful voice in creating equal access to capital. Now in her role as president and chief operating officer of the Skoll Foundation, she continues to be in an extremely influential position, and she is doing everything she can to create lasting change.

CINDE'S STORY

In our extended interview, Cat took great delight in telling me the story of Cinde Dolphin. CNote helped support her as a first-time entrepreneur based in Sacramento, California. Cinde is a four-time cancer survivor, who has been in and out of the hospital for years. During one of her earliest surgeries, the thing she realized she was most sick of was her drainage tube. If you have ever been operated on, you know that for sanitary and safety reasons, the doctors will usually put a tube inside of you to drain fluid so that it doesn't stay close to your wound. The tube comes with a pouch to carry around the excess fluid and, as Cinde expressed, "it is completely dehumanizing. The nurses often safety pin it to your gown and the whole thing just feels so undignified." Cinde decided she was going to do something about it, so she created KILI pouches that hold the fluid bag. Unlike the coarse plastic and paper, they are soft, look pretty, and are nice to wear.

Such a small device was bringing a sense of dignity back to cancer patients. Cinde started by making the pouch for herself, then several doctors and nurses asked her if they could buy them because they had several patients who had experienced the same thing. As often happens with small businesses, Cinde started making the pouches for people and couldn't keep up with demand. She wanted to start a business and went to her local bank for a loan.

As a first-time entrepreneur asking for a small loan, like many women, Cinde was denied. One 2019 study by HSBC Private Banking Investment reported by Sandeep Sandeep Soni for *The Financial Express*, claimed 50 percent of female entrepreneurs globally are denied funding from investors. In another study from 2019, a Bank of America survey said, "only 42 percent of female respondents said that women have equal access to capital," and 24 percent said they thought they would never have equal access.

Fortunately, Cinde didn't stop there. Instead, she went to her local CDFI, where she completed the same application for a loan request. This time, she was approved, and not only did they approve her for the loan, but they also gave her free technical assistance and business coaching. So Cinde gets her loan and starts making the pouches, then realizes she is managing all parts of the supply chain. She is buying materials, threading the fabric, selling, and shipping. She really wants to expand her supply chain. Now the story gets even more interesting.

What people didn't know about Cinde was that she was a big hiker. Mount Kilimanjaro was her passion and she would travel there any time she was healthy and could go. At the base of Mount Kilimanjaro are a group of women who are excellent at sewing. Over the years, she got to know this group of women. All of them had always struggled for income. They knew if they could get more income, they would be able to do tremendous things like send their daughters to school for the first time. So what did Cinde do? She included these women sewers at the base of Mount Kilimanjaro in her supply chain.

So today when you buy a KILI product, not only are you supporting this wonderful entrepreneur who's bringing back dignity to cancer survivors, but you're also helping send young girls to school in Africa. This is the story of investing in women and the power of putting money to work with women. There is no shortage of smart people who have the ideas and abilities like Cinde Dolphin and want to do good things. Capital flowing in their direction in a sufficient way is lacking. This is what Cat, and her work with CNote are helping to create.

As empowered women, if we have hard earned cash to invest, let's put our money to work in the hands of those who can create change in our communities and the world. From my experience, women entrepreneurs are interested in job creation, fair wages, being responsible business owners, and building something lasting that matters. When we as women invest in them, our return on investment is likely to be higher and more meaningful to us.

In December 2020, CNote closed a $3 million funding round with investors supporting their mission to unlock access to investments in racial equity, economic justice, and gender equity and help close the wealth gap in underserved communities across America. According to a February 2021 article from Geri Stengel for *Forbes*, "notably, the group of investors are diverse. Both men and women, as well as people from different geographies, backgrounds, and ethnicities, lead the funds that have invested."

What a great example of a flywheel in action. I get excited about the world we will create and nurture with all that money women will invest. That's the world I want to be part of.

What to Take Away?

Access to capital and what we do with it as women is a fundamental driver of change. It's a tool that we can wield to not only make our money work for us, but to support women-led initiatives and companies that are creating a positive future for all.

#Reflect

When I spoke with Marla Blow, she encouraged me to share that we ought to feel just as entitled to "play and participate" with our money as our male equivalents do. We do indeed have as much ability to use our money in ways that are meaningful for us, and for the environment around us, if we would only begin. It doesn't mean that we need to be rich when we start off, we can put our money to good use even in small ways to work for us and for others.

#Do

Raise the topic of money often. I know it's a hard one, but if we don't have more familiarity about it, then it will always be a difficult "money" conversation. Start with a close female friend and ask her if you can talk about your financials. Maybe start with what you are earning, what you would like to do with any savings, and ask her to do the same. Men talk about money, investing, and business all the time. They learn what's good and what's interesting, and they are happy to share their investments. More on this in the next chapter.

#Remember

Take a moment to also continue to empower yourself about money through knowledge and action. We are each 100 percent responsible for our money, and financial well-being, and the example you set will be a model for others.

CHAPTER 10

THE LAST TABOO

—

*Women belong in all places where
decisions are being made.*

—JUSTICE RUTH BADER GINSBURG

In the fall of 2020, we lost one of the greatest champions of women who had ever lived, Supreme Court Justice Ruth Bader Ginsberg. Shock waves rippled through the US as we absorbed the probable repercussions of her death. As we faced down one of the biggest challenges in a generation, losing one of our gender justice heroines felt like we had lost some of our armor, some of our protection.

Dubbed "The Notorious R.B.G." for her liberal and outspoken viewpoint, in 2018, NPR's Nina Totenburg explained that in her later years she became a pop culture icon as a strong, hard-working female leader, inspiring books and movies, and little girls who dressed up as her at Halloween. Her legacy is long. Her vote helped legalize same sex marriages in all fifty states, usher in gender equality provisions for equal pay, and protect pregnant women in the workplace. Through her eighty-seven years of life, she was a trailblazer, a fighter, and a fierce advocate for gender equality and women's rights.

The Equal Credit Opportunity Act was one of the little-known and far-reaching rulings R.B.G. paved the way for. Thankfully, it's not something we have to think about any longer. But before this time, as Erin El Issa chronicled in "Women and Credit Through the Decades" for NerdWallet in 2020, banks required single, widowed, or divorced women to bring a man along to cosign any credit application, regardless of their income. They would also discount the value of those wages when considering how much credit to grant by as much as 50 percent. Furthermore, many banks would still not issue credit to a woman without her husband's signature. This meant that until 1974, women couldn't get access to a loan or a mortgage without the direct approval of a male cosigner.

In talking about her own experiences, Gloria Feldt—feminist author and former president of Planned Parenthood—has been quoted by coauthors Sara M. Moniuszko, Maria Puente, and Veronica Bravo for *USA Today* in 2020, "I had been employed full time for several years, and was earning more than my ex. I went to buy a car and couldn't get a loan without my husband's signature. That was my tipping point to feminist activism." Thanks to R.B.G., men were no longer the sole breadwinners. Women were free to earn and spend their own money, as well as borrow it if they wanted to.

While this critical legislation is rarely referenced, the fact it took until 1974 for women to gain full control over their finances and investments still holds impact today. In my interview with Sophie McNaught, founder of The Shed—a community organization that inspires and educates women to take control of their finances—she mused, "just imagine, there are enormous barriers that your own mother would have faced, and that would influence the way that you've been raised to think about investing and wealth accumulation." Our parent's relationship with money is critical to our relationship with money, especially for women.

As Cat Berman is focused on creating tools to advance women's access to investing and capital, addressing our own relationship—and often embarrassment and fear of money—is a critical piece of the equation. Just like anything that was once new to us, when we increase our familiarity with money and investing, our confidence and abilities will grow.

WOMEN ARE ACTUALLY GREAT WITH MONEY

Sophie McNaught, who is also the director of corporate ventures for Fintech Lead at Silicon Valley Bank, shared with me that women are actually more often than not good with money, more than they realize. She explained, "we are good at keeping track of spending, budgeting, and working within constraints. It's what we've been expected to do for years, and we are very resourceful." As she spoke, I thought back to growing up in the UK with a backdrop of miners' strikes, bread shortages, and my mum making what little money we had go pretty far. She had clipped coupons out of the newspaper and saved a one-pound grocery stamp each week for the holidays. It was true I had seen budgeting and resourcefulness firsthand, and there was also a complete vacancy where my mum handed all investment decisions over to my dad. We were good with money until we had to trust giving it to someone else to take care of.

Fast forward forty years, now 47 percent of women hold the reins of their household finances. However, "we are still struggling to make progress with financial confidence, and decision making," according to the 2019 Women, Money and Power Study from Allianz Life. In the report, Aimee Lynn Johnson, vice president of financial planning strategies at Allianz Life says, "There is a lot of discussion on female empowerment and the accomplishments women are making. [...] But the disconnect between these accomplishments and the lack of financial confidence suggests those conversations need to refocus on female financial empowerment."

Sophie agreed completely, "The key part we've been missing and haven't quite caught up to, is the investing part of the equation. This is the missing piece to get to genuine wealth creation for women." And that's what Sophie and The Shed are solving for.

Her idea started when she noticed the men she had gone through university with were investing, but none of her girlfriends were. She started hosting Friday afternoon wine and cheese finance sessions at her apartment. She got an overwhelming response and things quickly expanded. Sophie went on to host regular gatherings every few weeks covering lots of financial topics. She brought in different guests like a wealth advisor or psychologist who would talk about the way money links to mental health or the way it is relevant in relationships. Sophie's idea was "if there's no appropriate place to talk about money, but everyone actually does want to talk about it. Well, I can create that place." I loved this simple and intimate idea that created a safe container for women to learn and share.

For women to achieve true empowerment, it is essential for the financial literacy gap to close. Education really is the key and the earlier we start the better. Today, according to The Shed's mission web page in 2021, "only 29 percent of girls are taught about investing, as opposed to 41 percent of boys." Sophie went on to explain that women often feel they need to perfectly understand financial mechanisms before they are willing to invest, but when they speak with other women investors and learn about their experience, their confidence and curiosity soar, and they are willing to experiment.

Personally, finances have always been a taboo subject for me. I felt I was terrible at math and have struggled to understand how to best invest. As I took the time to better educate myself and learn more about what the women around me were doing and why it mattered, it not only got me interested but also made me realize how important it was to take my future into my own hands. Discussing, sharing, and celebrating together allows women to build true financial confidence, gaining the knowledge and experience to help us put our hard-earned money to work.

Another woman seeking to buck the trend with female investing is Kristin Hull. She is a former educator and now the founder and CEO of Nia Impact Capital, which is based in Oakland, California. In 2019, she completed another twelve months of market-beating performance for her gender-lens investment portfolio company. They aim to earn financial returns and address gender disparities by investing in companies with a higher representation of women on their boards or in senior management positions. It makes great financial sense, as McKinsey's Diversity Matters report already showed in 2015, that companies with more diverse teams are 35 percent more likely to have financial returns above their respective national industry medians.

In 2019, Leslie P. Norton at *Barron's* wrote about Kristin's incredible feat as a gender-lens investor. According to her, she "is one of its best practitioners." She went on to quote more on Nia's 2019 performance, "During the first quarter, the Nia account returned 17.3 percent, beating the S&P 500 index's 13.7 percent and the MSCI ACWI's 12.4 percent." Apparently, that's shockingly good.

If you are anything like me, I might as well have shared those statistics with you in Russian. That's the rub that Kristin and I talk about. Women call her all the time, and say something to the effect, "I'm so ashamed. I don't know how to handle my money. I want to learn, but when we talk, please don't think I'm an idiot!" Kristin went on to share that literally the night before our interview, she had spoken with a highly successful court judge based in Santa Cruz County, California. "She's a badass! Like totally amazing, she's a criminal justice lawyer, she has a publicly held office, and she's feeling ashamed about not knowing how to do her investing."

> ## "Women empowering women is about me sharing every single thing I can to better educate women on how to best manage their money."
>
> —KRISTIN HULL

I breathed a sigh of relief as Kristin finished explaining, at that point. I was also ready to confide with Kristin that I had opened our interview with a pretty lame question, and I had been dreading the call. I did my preparation research on Kristin, her company Nia Impact, and read a number of financial articles about her success, most of which I was having trouble understanding. I felt exactly the same as the majority of her clients and other women in the world when it came to finances. I felt like a fool.

YOU ARE NOT ALONE

"That's exactly it!" Kristin, went on with her natural grace and kind way of speaking and connecting. Her nurturing tone, quickly put me at ease as she let me know I was not alone in my lack of understanding about what money does to us. "Women are ashamed when they don't have as much money as their male colleagues and family members, and equally so when they do." There's that double bind for women at play once again.

Kristin saw this squarely as the patriarchy at work, "The men aren't sitting at home feeling insecure, and full of shame. They're also the ones not left out of the conversation." She recounted an equally funny and heartbreaking story about a recent conversation she had with a Black colleague. It had been some time since they had last spoken, and Kristin shared that she is trying to empower women and people of color through her work at Nia Impact. Her friend inquired, "Wait, you all don't know about finance?" Kristin said, no, white women don't know about finance. Her friend went on to lament, she had thought that they were the ones who were left out. She knew Black women didn't know about finance, but she had no idea white women also didn't know. I felt my heart break as we spoke.

Kristin was confirming what Sophie had shared about the effects of the lack of financial education on "every single woman, every age, in every demographic, in every country."

Once women do get over their initial shame and hesitation of investing, however, we connect the dots easily, and we want more. Organizations like Nia are changing the landscape for women investors. They manage portfolios of women-for-ward and woman-led companies, empowering their female clients to make confident financial decisions based on their values. What's more, when women do invest, they consistently outperform their male counterparts, which could leave them with hundreds of thousands of dollars more at retirement, according to Fidelity Investments in 2017.

Kristin also writes a blog called, *Money Doula*. She told me how this metaphor of birthing wealth with all its struggles deeply resonates with women, and that amusingly men have no idea what it is! A doula is a trained professional who provides emotional and informational support to a mother before, during, and after childbirth. The *Money Doula* similarly provides information, education, and support in a woman's financial journey to align their assets with their personal values. Money certainly can feel as uncomfortable and terrifying as giving birth, and when we get past the initial pain, the joys and achievements on your investments can be life changing.

Kristin's female investors have significant wealth to invest with a $100k minimum investment (the Nia Impact account has $100 million in assets, as of 2019 *Barron's* Abby Schultz reported). She recalls asking her potential clients, "Did you know that your bank is funding fossil fuel projects and you could put it in a local bank that goes toward women-owned businesses, and be just as secure and just as safe, and maybe get even a little bit higher return?" When you put it like that, Kristin smiled, "It's a no-brainer." It's not only about pure investor returns for women, when we have financial literacy and control, we are more likely to make investments back into our local communities. In the developing world, The World Economic Forum's Tae Yoo described in 2014, women are reported to reinvest 90 percent of their income back into their families and communities. We donate more to charities too. In a 2016 *Wall Street Journal* study, Debra Mesch explained, "baby-boomer and older women gave 89 percent more to charity than men their age."

"Empowering women really *is* my theory of change. When we have women understand their finances and act with intention, we›re going to have a completely different economy," Kristin passionately said. And with projections from Bankrate indicating that women will inherit 70 percent of future wealth over the course of the next two generations, it's exciting to imagine a world where women are really voting with their dollars and investing in the world they want to see.

Helping women invest their money and gain wealth is good for them and good for all of us. Women who do well, want to invest in other women and women-led companies that create change. Those companies perform better, which in turn creates more wealth to invest, and so on. That's a virtuous circle that women are waking up to, and now they can and want to get behind it. Money empowers more women. The system works, we only need more women in the system to get the equity circle around the world spinning bigger and faster.

Every investment has impact. Money is an enabler, it's fuel, and it's power. It's waiting for us to do good with it!

What to Take Away?

Our relationship with money is often not a relationship at all. When we create more environments where women can talk freely about money without shame and judgment, we increase the possibility of putting it to work not only for ourselves but as a powerful vehicle to affect change. When more wealth is amassed, spent, or invested by women, the world will look very different.

#Do

Actually talk about money. It's one of the last big taboos for women. When we have active and intentional conversations about it, we create a familiarity and comfort level to gain greater confidence and skills. When you initiate a conversation about money, know you are helping to change our culture of embarrassment about the subject. Your courage to approach this taboo topic with openness will help you and other women become more active in creating financial awareness, understanding, and security.

#Remember

Encourage another woman to engage with her disposable income actively. As Sophie shared with me, "you are engaging with it, whether you're being deliberate about it or not. Your inaction is a decision. Your willful blindness is leading to an outcome. It just might not be the outcome that you want." Help someone see that money is a powerful tool, and it can now be invested to create so much good in the world while creating a return on investment for them.

#Do

Taking time every week or even every day to learn about money is like working out, if we haven't made time for ourselves, it simply won't happen. Encouraging the women around us, especially younger women, to make time for learning about their money is so important. It could be as simple as a weekly thirty-minute meeting to familiarize herself with her bank accounts and spending. All the way to using that time to research financial products, hiring a financial advisor, or sitting down with you to talk about your finances together.

CHAPTER 11

THE FINAL FRONTIER

---

*The secret of change is to focus all
of your energy, not on fighting the
old, but on building the new.*

—SOCRATES

Do you know a woman who has served on the board of a for-profit business? If you do, you are a rarity—and so is she. Getting a position on a board remains as elusive for women as a covert mission you've never heard of. We still need to shatter so many glass ceilings, but the boardroom is a place where few women have rarely seen the inside to even know where to start. The board is the ultimate decision-maker inside a company and is even more important than the CEO. It's critical that women are serving on boards and gaining access to influence and leverage.

One woman working to change all that is Jocelyn Mangan, founder of Him for Her—a social impact venture aimed at accelerating gender diversity in the boardroom. According to Ann Shepherd and Gené Teare, sharing the Him for Her and Crunchbase 2020 Study of Gender Diversity on Private Company Boards, only 23 percent of the top three thousand US publicly traded companies have women on their boards and only 11 percent of women in private companies.

Jocelyn had birthed the idea for her organization during her tenure as a fellow at the Aspen Henry Crown Fellowship. Passionate about women at work, she focused her fellowship on women's representation in the boardroom and started analyzing the data. Needless to say, she told me, it was abysmal. As a former product executive at large tech companies like Ticketmaster and OpenTable, Jocelyn set out trying to better understand why women have been absent from one of the most important rooms in business for so long.

IT'S NOT A PIPELINE PROBLEM

"I interviewed ninety male leaders to learn more about the space, how they think about boards, and board recruitment," Jocelyn shared, "I wanted to discover what were the universal truths that shaped their mindset and approach. Firstly, I have to say, all the men I interviewed told me they wanted to help make their boards more diverse, but they didn't know how to start."

Jocelyn continued, "Secondly, when I asked how they found their last board member, they gave me a personal network story." That's when she understood boards are something that happens within personal networks and her idea for

Him for Her got started in earnest. If all women are not prominently in male board members' direct relationships and trusted circles, they are not likely to tap us to become a new board member. Hundreds of women are board-ready, Jocelyn explained.

> "It's not a pipeline problem.
> It's a network issue."
>
> —JOCELYN MANGAN

Today, according to their website, Him for Her has "built a referral-only talent network of 3,000+ board-ready women, a third of whom are women of color, and delivered free board-referral lists to six hundred and growing companies ranging from start-ups to S&P 100." Since its founding in 2018, Jocelyn and her team have been working to bridge the network gap between board-ready women and the people in the boardroom today. I had been introduced to Jocelyn about six months before our interview by a woman my organization had supported. She thought Jocelyn and I should get to know each other. As part of that first call, I ended up becoming one of those 3,000+ women she has in her board-ready network.

In my own universe, boards have also been a mystery. I have served as an "advisory board member" where each month I have regularly offered advice one-to-one with a founder or executive. The roles were always without any decision-making powers and did not come with any salary or payment. All of the organizations where I have served as an advisor were nonprofits or social ventures. I finally became a board director with key fiduciary duties and governance responsibilities when I founded my own organization, The Coaching Fellowship, which is also a nonprofit. I would appear to squarely fit the description of most women who are executives—highly experienced—and I was also a founder four times. However, I have never been asked or interviewed to join the corporate board of a for-profit company.

Jocelyn told me the tide is turning though, with more companies looking to increase the number of women on their board. It makes good business sense economically for the company and its shareholders. A 2014 report by the Credit Suisse Research Institute discovered that companies with one or more women on the board delivered higher average returns on equity, lower net debt equity, and better average growth. Furthermore, it's not just the right thing to do, but leads to better and safer products. Research cited by Spencer Jakab for *The Wall Street Journal* in 2020, has shown that the presence of women on a pharmaceutical firm's board results in faster recalls of products with severe problems, meaning with more women on boards, there are fewer dangerous products on the market.

More countries and organizations are waking up to these facts and now moving to mandate board numbers to help close the gender gap. As recorded by Laurel Wamsley for NPR in 2018, California was a pioneer when it became the first US state to require a minimum number of women directors for its publicly traded firms headquartered there in 2018. In 2020, Goldman Sachs announced that it will no longer take companies public unless they have at least one non-white male board member; and Nasdaq, at the end of 2020, submitted a proposal requiring listed companies to have at least two diverse directors, including one self-identifying woman and one self-identifying underrepresented minority or LGBTQ+. According to Ann Shepherd and Gené Teare, the latest Him for Her and Crunchbase annual Study of Gender Diversity on Private Company Boards from March 2021, goes on to show that despite some progress, "women remain absent from half of private company boards, lagging dramatically behind public companies."

Jocelyn is not deterred, however, she revels in sharing the story of a woman she helped support via her network board bridge. Jocelyn recounted the story of the first-time CFO of a Hollywood-based business she met, "I just loved her energy and thought she would be a great board member. I asked her to join one of our LA dinners where I brought together a great table of people." Over the course of the following year, Liz Jenkins reached back out to Jocelyn to thank her because she had met two different people at that dinner and landed two board seats.

According to Shama Hyder, writing for *Inc Magazine* in 2019, "only one in twenty-five senior leaders is a woman of color." Liz, as a Black woman executive, is squarely in the minority, and even more so, as a Black female board member, where Him for Her reports "only 3 percent of private company board seats are held by women of color."

When I spoke with Liz, it was clear why she had been quickly tapped to join those boards, one publicly traded. She is a straight talking, smart powerhouse of making change happen. Her energy is infectious, her laugh lights you up, and she is a fierce champion of women and diversity. It's clear that anyone who met Liz would want to find a way to keep her close by. The trouble was getting to meet people like her in the first place.

Liz is on the executive team of Hello Sunshine, Reese Witherspoon's media company, which aims to change the narrative for women by putting them at the center of every story they create where her role expanded recently to COO. She had always believed it would take years to get on a board.

"That's what everyone tells you. It also might never happen, and if it does, you have to be very patient," she told me. Liz had been shocked to get a call from two of the guests at the Los Angeles dinner, and even more so when they engaged her in conversation about a board position. These were people outside of Liz's circle, and if it wasn't for the invitation from Jocelyn, she knew she would never have met them otherwise.

WOMEN EQUAL MORE WOMEN

"I live in the world of women empowering women every day right now. We're onboarding a hundred women a month at Him for Her, and many of those referrals come from women to women. That tells me the flywheel is turning already," Jocelyn explained. Just as she had said, there are thousands of board-ready women, boards just don't know how to meet them.

When women join boards, it's a valuable opportunity for personal and professional growth, and it can ultimately help fuel career advancement. Be that strengthening credibility and reputation, increasing visibility, expanding network and inner circle, or honing a new industry, leadership, and management skill. Board positions are a hallmark of success. Whether the role is for a nonprofit, start-up, or corporation, board experience will help sharpen your skills, gain further exposure, and signal you are ready for more.

In addition to this and the benefits women on boards bring to a company's bottom line, women can help promote diversity directly within the board they are serving. A 2020 study from J. Yo-Jud Cheng and Boris Groysberg for MIT Sloan, showed that initial investment in recruiting women directors could create a positive feedback loop that paved the way for boards' future diversity and capacity for supporting long-term innovation and creativity. Furthermore, it's critical that different stakeholders have different perspectives to push boundaries and seek paths that a homogeneous board would otherwise forego. Lastly, a governing board really ought to more closely reflect the demographics of their employees and customer base.

Part of the challenge with boards is that they are stuck in a historical construct that has existed for a long time. As business models evolve and a company's products, mission, and focus change, it's important that boards change too. Jocelyn likes to call what's needed "systemic innovation." She doesn't think boards will change quickly, but she does think that as more diverse people join boards and bring new energy and ways of seeing and doing, "that more people will become aware of what their board is, and then those trends will start to move in the right direction."

When board rooms are no longer the hallowed ground where we dare not tread, and when the board of directors are no longer separated from the very company they are there to help advise, then they can truly govern from a place of full awareness and choice. Then they can make more equitable decisions and open a window to more opportunities and growth.

When women join boards, the potential for everyone and everything increases. That's why it's critical to have women like Jocelyn bridge the network gap until more empowered women can bring more empowered women into the room.

What to Take Away?

Women and board service is a rare combination but one that is gathering steam. Awareness—and in some cases, mandates—are driving change in one of the last areas to make the invisible visible and accessible. More women are joining boards and affecting change at the board level, which means they will now never go back to being men-only affairs. The final curtain is falling and with women at the true center of decision-making and power for an organization, we have the opportunity to unlock the potential for a fairer and equitable world.

#Do

Understanding boards is essential for all of us. Let's educate ourselves and others on the importance of putting oneself forward for a board position. That means we need to continue to grow our network, and say yes to opportunities to meet new people. As a board advisor or board director, each experience helps grow our confidence, experience, and stature. Our influence on that board will bring other women and voices forward, which could have a significant impact on not only the organization, but the world.

#Remember

Ask men for help. In this case, we sincerely need the help of our male colleagues because there are so few women on boards and so few board positions that become open. It's important to raise the topic of board diversity within our network, to the CEOs we know, and to any male board members and executives in our circle. There is a misbelief that there are not enough board-ready women, but as Jocelyn has shown, we are ready, we are simply not being asked. Let's be sure to introduce ourselves and other women to the male decision-makers and influencers in our midst.

#Do

Another way to help women gain basic board skills is to create one for your area of responsibility. If you run a marketing division, or have remit for a country or region, why not consider recruiting some volunteer advisors to help you better understand a new market, product fit, and new industry? You will gain the wealth of their expertise and knowledge, and they will have an advisory position to reference as well as new skills to boot.

CHAPTER 12

THE TROUBLEMAKING INDIVIDUAL

If people are doubting how far you can go,
go so far that you can't hear them anymore.

—MICHELE RUIZ

The year of 2020 will go down as a year of devastation and reckoning because of COVID-19. However, when it came to US Initial Public Offerings, it was a bumper year with Alyson Shontell from Business Insider reporting 442 companies filing to go IPO. That amounted to 201 more than in 2019, which made scores of founders into millionaires overnight—and quite a few billionaires too. How many of those were led by women? Only four. In fact, since the New York Stock Exchange was founded in 1817, Samantha Kelly from the Story Exchange has documented there have been thousands of publicly traded companies, but only thirty-one have involved women from the beginning.

There have been some signs of change, albeit numbers are still drastically low. In February 2021, Whitney Wolfe Herd became the youngest female founder and CEO—at the age of thirty-one—to make an initial public offering. As Nicole Laporte in Fast Company described, she exceeded expectations to raise $2.1 billion with her women friendly dating company, Bumble. She also did so "with a board that's 73 percent women, which is completely unprecedented in technology," says Clare O'Connor, Bumble's head of editorial content. She became the youngest self-made female billionaire in the world, with a baby on her hip to boot. Whitney is the role model we have been waiting for and more are following.

According to Zoe Bernard at The Information, in 2021 there are several more women poised to take their high-valuation companies public in the next few years. They include Anne Wojcicki (cofounder of 23andMe), Sarah Friar (CEO at Nextdoor), and Melanie Perkins (CEO of Canva), among others. It's certainly encouraging to see, but numbers of women-led companies fall still desperately short of what's needed to reach any kind of parity with those led by men. An April 2020 analysis of securities filings by women's venture organization All Raise, as referenced by Bernard, claims of the $334.8 billion in wealth generated by the past decade's top ten tech IPOs, 92 percent was held by principal shareholders who were men.

These numbers are critical because those who earn significant wealth also get to decide where to invest their extensive assets, and that tends to be back into companies and people who look a lot like them. So if only men are taking their companies public, gaining untold wealth, and investing back into their existing networks who are men, it's even tougher for women to break into getting their company funded.

A PIONEER IN SUPPORTING WOMEN FOUNDERS

That's something that Sharon Vosmek knows all too well. She has led Astia as their CEO for the past fourteen years as the organization works to help high-growth companies led by women succeed. I was privileged to join Astia as an Entrepreneur in Residence in 2012, where Sharon and the Astia community helped me hone my own business concept and next steps. Astia has been a pioneer in supporting women founders starting more than twenty years ago. Up until the past few years, it had been focused on helping them gain leverage by creating access to skills, network, and some early-stage investment capital through Astia Angels.

In my interview with Sharon, we caught up on what had changed at Astia and where her focus is today. "After ten years of working non-stop to help women succeed, we realized the market just wasn't moving." Women were building successful companies, but they were only able to grow so big—the missing element was funding. According to a 2016 explorative study by Abdulwahab Bin Shmailan comparing the characteristics of male and female entrepreneurs, this lack of start-up capital affects the survival rates of female-owned businesses and their ability to scale.

When I first met Sharon almost a decade ago, she would tell me she wanted Astia to be so successful that she would be out of a job. If that was the case, women founders would no longer need the kind of support Astia was providing because many more women founders would be exiting their companies. Alas, Sharon explained, "We found best in class entrepreneurs, helped them access expertise, and prepared them for investment, only to then see them fall off a cliff through no fault of their own. VCs were just unwilling or unable to invest in women."

Sharon set about building a new solution and moved Astia to focus purely on the missing ingredient, providing investment capital for its female founders themselves. In February 2021, as described on their website, they launched a "$100M early-stage venture fund aimed at addressing the extraordinary disparity in funding for companies that include women in founding or executive roles." The problem women are facing is indeed extraordinary. One HSBC Private Banking 2019 study referenced by Sandeep Soni for *The Financial Express*, reported that half of the world's female entrepreneurs are denied funding and a third face gender bias from investors. In 2020, Crunchbase figures show that venture funding for US women-led start-ups amounted to a mere 2.3 percent.

Systemic issues also include the sheer effort, burden, and labor involved for women to raise capital. Sharon shared a story about one company she supported that had raised $3 million from ninety investors. It took 245 days to close, versus the typical 161 days it takes a male-founded start-up. Then there's the blatant sexism that comes into play during the fundraising process when women are often asked questions about their family circumstances, their credibility as business leaders, and in some cases face direct sexual harassment as Tracy Chou shared in Chapter 4.

One highly successful entrepreneur who faced her own funding challenges is Kathryn Minshew, the thirty-five-year-old cofounder of The Muse—an online career resource with tens of millions of customers. Kathryn and I worked together when she took part in The Coaching Fellowship as her organization took off like a rocket ship in 2015. Since she founded The Muse in 2011, Kathryn has raised more than $28 million dollars, but the journey wasn't easy. Kathryn told me she experienced many sexist encounters with venture capitalists. "They were very dismissive. I was twenty-five when I started the business and even though we were growing fast, somebody would pat me on the head and tell me I seemed like too nice of a little girl to start a business. It was frustrating."

The thing that helped Kathryn to keep going and not give up was a strong network of women around her. Kathryn had been invited to join theLi.st, an all-female email listserv started by journalists Rachel Sklar and Glynnis MacNicol. The group consisting of female founders would "swap intel on who was grabby in pitch meetings, who was dismissive, and who was supportive," shared Kathryn. It had been critically helpful in the early days of her founding journey and even ended up helping her meet three female seed investors. "The first time I appeared on television representing my company, it was because of theLi.st," Kathryn shared in a 2017 *Inc Magazine* article with Jessica Bennett, and went on to explain how she "met another executive I admired through theLi. st. She became an adviser and, three years later, is now an executive at my company."

Women need women as supporters, champions, and funders, and none more so than women of color. If the funding challenges are harrowing for white women founders and the eventual investments paltry, spare a moment to consider the realities for women of color who are incidentally the fastest growing US entrepreneurial demographic, according to Ruth Umoh in 2020 for Forbes Women. Sharon Vosmek explained to me her personal experiences of supporting woman of color founders, "Once Astia has made an investment, it takes on average sixty-plus introductions for us to help that woman of color raise additional capital, whereas it typically takes five introductions to complete a round of follow-on funding for white founders. And then still we struggle to get the deal done." She goes on, "everyone wants to help be a mentor and advisor, but I say to people if you really want to help, then the next step is to dare to write a check." Amen to that.

It's hard to understand why more women do not get funded when evidence clearly points to women-led start-ups being more likely to succeed and being decidedly better financial investments, as confirmed by a 2018 Boston Consulting Group analysis. Whether due to the additional hurdles women founders must traverse to win funding, grow their businesses out of the gate, and be cash flow positive, they are indeed "made" into being the better and more resilient entrepreneurs.

However, as Leah Fessler reports in her 2018 Quartz article, with 92 percent of partners at the biggest VC firms in the US being men and controlling "an outsize proportion of a firm's investment decisions, women founders are at a serious disadvantage." This all changes when women founders meet women investors. According to Pam Kostka, CEO of All Raise in 2020, while only 12 percent of decision-makers at VC firms are women, and most firms still don't have a single female partner, when women venture capitalists do make the decisions, they're twice as likely to invest in female founding teams.

WOMEN INVESTORS ARE THE KEY

That's something Ann Cairns, executive vice chair at Mastercard who was a lead investor in Astia's first venture fund, understands and is excited to nurture. As she shared in their investment announcement, "Too much of our world was designed without women in mind—and without women involved. When women and underrepresented groups are at the leadership table, these teams outperform for customers, investors, and companies." Furthermore, there's a growing number of organizations seeking to fund women-owned businesses and also seeking to revolutionize how the funding component actually works.

Vicky Saunders created SheEO in 2015 as a way to help women build the business they want to build and on their own terms. As Vicki explains on the SheEO website, "In order to get to the new solutions for the world's most pressing social issues; we need to shed our 'winner takes all culture' that has resulted in five men having the same wealth as half the planet! Fifty-one percent of the population are women, yet we receive 2.2 percent of the capital. This is statistically impossible without massive bias designed into our systems and structures." There are now more than six thousand SheEO Activators, women contributing to a perpetual fund that distributes 0 percent loans to women-led ventures. They are upending Wall Street and creating a funding mechanism that is accessible to many more women.

> "We are not here to win.
> We are here to transform."
>
> —VICKY SAUNDERS

In every way, women-owned businesses contribute to the good of the economy, the workforce, and the world. According to an analysis by Kauffman Fellows, a program designed to accelerate entrepreneurs' success, "women-run businesses with a female founder fill their staffs with two and a half times more women, and companies with a female founder *and* a female executive hire six times more women." So it would seem that one of the fastest ways to achieve gender equality is to close the entrepreneurial gap and support more women founders. Women leading and building businesses on their own terms are helping all people create momentum and rise.

American playwright and novelist, Natalie Clifford Barney, once said, "Entrepreneurship is the last refuge of the troublemaking individual." And when I see women like Vicky Saunders, Sharon Vosmek, or Cat Berman at CNote creating change by building businesses differently, I see a lot of good troublemaking happening. I see women entrepreneurs reimagining how we transform every segment of society to be fairer and more equitable, all while building highly successful and far-reaching global businesses.

Founding is about starting and making something new. It's a crucible of ideas and ideals, a place where people come together to build something that never existed before. Women founders are the brave ones who are picking up the hard problems to solve using business as the tip of the spear, and in their wake, they are creating a wind of change that can lift us all.

What to Take Away?

When women build businesses, they care as deeply about the impact they make, as much as the profits. Success to these pioneers also means taking care of their customers, employees, and community. And with women led companies focused more often than not on real-world problems, women are some of the strongest entrepreneurs working to solve our grand systemic challenges. They are the ones daring to innovate to create the world we want to see, and their empowering businesses are creating an opportunity for all of us.

#Reflect

Realize when something is no longer working, try shifting the goalposts. When Sharon honestly and critically reviewed the impact of Astia over the past ten years, she saw they had worked hard and created change, but it hadn't been enough to create lasting impact. It's important to review what we are doing often and see where we can create the most leverage. It's also critical to think creatively without the binds of long-established rules so new solutions can be found.

#Remember

Leverage our network and relationships. Back to the chapters on women and networking, we can support one another as women to keep going and not give up. When we come together, en masse, we can unleash a torrent of energy, action, and momentum. Whether we are supporting female entrepreneurs, work colleagues, friends, and sisters, when we empower another woman in big and small ways, we are contributing to the greater good for all of us.

#Do

Vote with our feet. When we buy products and services from women-owned businesses, we are choosing not to help only a handful of individuals, but choosing a conscious action that will be part of changing the entire system. Products, people, power, wherever we put our dollars has an impact.

PART II

THE TEN KEYS TO UNLOCK THE POTENTIAL OF ALL WOMEN

INTRODUCTION
TO PART II

Every national team and every athlete going to the Olympic Games wants to win the gold medal, that's focusing on the goal. But according to James Clear, author of the book *Atomic Habits*, the goal doesn't distinguish us, it's also about who we are in relation to that goal. If we want to actually lock in a habit that will ultimately create systems change, we have to focus on the system to achieve the goal.

For example, James says, if you want to quit smoking, saying "I gave up cigarettes" when someone offers you a smoke, is weaker than saying "I'm not a smoker." What seems like a subtle language change is actually working on a deeper level as it ties directly into our personality and therefore our identity. We are more likely to keep doing something if we see ourselves as the embodiment of the action, instead of simply a vessel carrying out a goal. Rather, like a runner who sees themselves as an athlete will run more often—and likely faster, and longer too—compared to someone who doesn't take on the personality of an athlete and just runs "to stay fit."

So what does that mean for us in the context of creating systemic change and gender equality?

By choosing to identify ourselves as female activists, we are more likely to take action or take multiple actions. Keep doing it in the face of adversity and encourage others to do the same. That's not saying that you haven't been supporting and empowering women before now. Rather, when we make a switch to embrace and embody female activism as part of our personality and identity, we will seek ways every day to fulfill our way of being that person in the world.

If you want to take more action, and I imagine you do, then claiming your role as feminist or activist—whatever works best for you—will go a long way to deepening and forwarding your own role to play.

What comes next are the ten keys I have identified from my interviews and working with young women leaders over the past decade. We can do them every single day to empower another woman. They are not difficult, and they do not require specialized knowledge.

You don't have to chain yourself to railings or fear retribution. At a first glance, you may think them small and unremarkable, but they are part of a quiet, steadfast revolution. A judo move that wasn't seen coming. A tidal wave of kinetic energy with women at the core. A sum of the parts working to win the ultimate goal of women being truly recognized, safe, and equal across the entire world.

Yes, of course, we need laws changed, we need people held accountable for abuses, and we need generational bias to be a thing of the past. We need all of those things. Every day, it is in our power to help women feel whole, powerful, and ready. We can keep them stepping forward and lifting them up high. We have a long way to go, and we are the solution. You know the adage "if you want something done right, do it yourself?" Yep, that's true in this case too.

The second part of this book will activate you to take progress for women into your own hands. Our goal is to reach gender equity within a generation. I challenge you to take on a handful of these keys to unlocking a woman's potential, starting today. Just like those Olympic athletes, practice them on a daily basis, celebrate yourself as an activist, and create collective change together, one step at a time. A hundred, a thousand, or a million tiny empowering steps is the only way everlasting and meaningful change will occur, and the way the gold medal is won.

Let's get started!

CHAPTER 13

KEY #1—JUST SAY YES

———

One of the simplest ways we can help another woman is just to say yes. Yes to an introduction. Yes to a thirty-minute call. Yes to giving some advice. Yes to any request within the realm of possibility. It might surprise you to know that your small yes could be the pathway to a big new job for her and a wage rise to boot. It could be the difference between a strategic project succeeding and failing, it could be the momentum she needed to not check out of the workforce, and keep going. When we say yes, we never truly know the full implication of what will follow. But one thing is true, by saying yes—you will create a shift in the universe for something good to happen.

So here's our first, quick, and easy key.

Just Say *Yes*!

Cat Berman from CNote shared this sage advice with me when I interviewed her for Chapter 9 on access to capital. It was toward the end of the call when I asked Cat something I have asked everyone who I interviewed for the book—What is the simplest thing we can do to help a fellow sister?

"Just say yes," Cat immediately said, her words hit me squarely in the chest, like I had never thought of that before. Her short and powerful response deeply touched me. By specifically helping another woman in your life, just saying yes becomes a meaningful positive action of solidarity and support. Furthermore, it's something achievable and even the smallest of actions may create the biggest of ripples. Remember Tracy Chou writing her 2013 blog post, "Where are the numbers?" and encouraging people to release the actual number of women in technology in their company? Her single action kicked off the diversity debate in Silicon Valley, which is still creating change many years later.

"One of my mantras is never say no to the invitation to support another woman," Cat shared with me. She explained it is important to make the time because we really don't know how hard it was for that woman to ask you for help. Often, we as women don't ask because we feel like we are burdening others, or are concerned we will be perceived as weak. Sometimes, we are simply overwhelmed, and don't even know where to begin to get help. So, by the time a woman has gotten to you, whether it was flat out asking you directly or she may have gotten someone to make that introduction email, it's likely she had to go through her own journey just to get to you.

Cat went on to tell me, "My personal belief is never say no to help another woman even if it's inconvenient, even if it's hard, even if you think you can't help. Because even if you give that person thirty minutes, and you may not be the door they need to open, but you could probably know the right door and make that connection for them." When she said it like that, I couldn't help but agree.

WHY SAYING YES IS HARD

So why do we say no? We often think we are not the right person to help, our expertise isn't good enough, we don't want to waste their time, or we don't have the power to help. It is not from a place of malice, but rather our own feeling of disempowerment. In a 2014 study referenced by *The Atlantic's* Katty Kay and Claire Shipman, half of female manager respondents reported self-doubt about their job performance and career. Imposter syndrome is real for many of us, and it strikes at any point in our career. In fact, according to Laura M. Newinski and Paul Knopp from KPMG in 2020, it's experienced by 75 percent of female executives.

The 2014 Katty Kay and Claire Shipman *Atlantic* article continues, "when women don't act, when we hesitate because we aren't sure, we hold ourselves back," and our lack of confidence leads to inaction. The article goes on to say what dooms us is not our actual ability to do well, but what holds us back is the choice we make not to try. This is, therefore, our work to do for ourselves, to allow ourselves to be seen as someone who *can* help someone else grow and be part of their success. By saying yes, we also get to work on our own value and worth; it is an empowering act for ourselves as well as others.

On the other hand, there is a perceived notion that women say yes too much, we have trouble with boundaries, and we take on too much. That can all be true, and it is something we need to keep working on, but I would challenge you to consider how many women are regularly asking you for help, my guess is very few. My team and I work with over three hundred young women leaders each year. Only a handful ever reach out beyond our program for help, and I always say yes. Some want to know how I built The Coaching Fellowship, and some seek me out for career advice. Maybe it takes a few weeks before I have time, but squeezing in twenty minutes to chat is never impossible. So let's also encourage women to ask for the help, and let them know it's okay to ask you.

A yes can also be so much more than the action you take. Saying yes also means you *see* that other woman, she exists, and is worthy of your help and support. As I've said, it might have taken a bunch of courage for her to reach out to you in the first place, and she likely thought she wouldn't even get a reply. So regardless of the thing you said you would do for her, just know by the simple act of saying yes, you will have already made something great happen.

And by the way, if your yes is actually a no, a "sorry I can't help right now, love what you are doing, keep going," or a "try me again in three months" also matters and means something for her. I get hundreds of emails each day, and I try to respond to them all. I know we all hate, hate, hate email, but a kind "good for you," a "thanks for letting me know," or a simple "wahoo" can make all the difference in letting her know her efforts were not in vain. So, if it's still a no, and you give her a warm reception, she might be ready to try knocking on the next door.

Let's also not forget how good saying yes feels. Research has also proved it's good for us! According to Dr. Christine Carter in a 2010 *Psychology Today* article, kinder people actually live longer and healthier lives. Additionally, their research says, "people who volunteer tend to experience fewer aches and pains," and "giving help to others protects overall health twice as much as aspirin protects against heart disease." So giving really is getting.

Something special happens when women support one another, whether we are sharing our wisdom, giving emotional or physical support through connections, and more, saying yes to lifting up a sister is good for everyone. And it feels great! Way to go to live more joy.

Where to start? Why not try committing to at least once a week saying yes to a woman who asked for help? If that doesn't feel like enough, seek out one woman in your life who you know needs help and just tell her you said yes to help anyway! One small action could amount to untold impact—especially if those small actions are magnified by the thousands.

Cat shared her rule with me pretty early on when I began writing this book, and I became deeply aware of the kind and generous acts of the women who said yes to making introductions and to my interview requests. Getting a "yes" also made me bolder with my next tasks and deepened my sense of sisterhood.

By bringing more awareness to saying yes, you will help more women more often. And you will build your own power, presence, and joy by supporting a woman on her path. That sense of cocreated potential is a powerful force for all of us.

By the way, these keys are prime lessons for all of us too. So make sure you are asking for help from others when you need it, remember your value and your worth, have fun, and let's get that flywheel turning.

YES, YES, YES!!

CHAPTER 14

KEY #2—TELL HER SHE IS READY

How many times have you heard a "I don't think I should," or a "I don't think I can," from a female friend or work colleague? If you are anything like me, the answer is too many times, and if I am honest, I would have to throw in a whole bunch of my own, "I just can't do that" statements. We've all been there. I've been there a lot, and believe me, writing a book will absolutely do that to you! Self-doubt is a cruel beast that strips away our brilliance and has us shine only a fraction of our light out there in the world. Yet, when we are encouraged, when someone believes in us and what we can make possible, then as women we really know how to move heaven and Earth. We are the champions of bearing pain, we are the endurance athletes of fitting everything into a single day, and we hold the wisdom of centuries of sisters in our bones. Women know how to show up, manifest change, and give their all. We are the solution and that requires us to believe we are the ones to make it happen.

So before that big opportunity comes along, let's all get into the habit, and

Tell Her She Is Ready!

It's a well touted fact that women need to feel 100 percent ready before they will act. This was famously unearthed by Hewlett-Packard almost a decade ago while conducting a study to get more women into key management positions. Their benchmark study referenced by Tara Sophia Mohr in the *Harvard Business Review* in 2014, showed that women working at HP applied for a promotion only when they believed they met 100 percent of the qualifications listed for the job. Men were happy to apply when they thought they could meet 60 percent of the job requirements. Behavioral data from Maria Ignatova sharing LinkedIn's Gender Insights Report in 2019, confirms ten years later, that those women still tend to screen themselves out of the conversation and "end up applying to 20 percent fewer jobs than men."

In a 2019 *New York Times* piece by Lisa Damour about the Hewlett-Packard study, they sum it up with the claim, "underqualified and underprepared men don't think twice about leaning in. Overqualified and overprepared, too many women still hold back. Women feel confident only when they are perfect." That's only half the truth though, women did not lack confidence in their abilities, rather, they did not apply for a job because they did not believe they met all the required qualifications, and thus would not get the job. Tara Sophia Mohr went on to explain in her *Harvard Business Review* article, 78 percent of the reasons why women chose not to apply for a role was actually connected to beliefs around the hiring process and following the "rules," and not about their inabilities.

So that's where you come in. We are so strongly socialized to follow the rules, another *Harvard Business Review* suggests, in part, our "success in school (relative to boys) arguably can be attributed to better rule following," but when it comes to our careers, this kind of conformity can keep us on the sidelines. When we see a woman expressing doubt, let's try to get to the bottom of what's really going on. Often inaction is mistaken for a lack of confidence, but as we're learning, it might be more a habit of following the rules. As Sally Stephanie Schriock, president of EMILY's List—the women's political action group—writes in her 2021 book, *Run to Win: Lessons in Leadership for Women Changing the World*, "one of the most important parts of knowing the lessons and unwritten rules is figuring out when you can and should break them."

Maria Ignatova, in the LinkedIn Gender Insights Report, went on to say, "the good news is that when women do apply to a job, they are 16 percent more likely than men to get hired. In fact, if the role is more senior than their current position, that number goes up to 18 percent." Women will acutely underestimate and undersell their skills and worth, but when they don't, they are highly likely to be successful. Help her see that what appears to be rules are often guides and encourage her to try giving it a go.

What's even more limiting than following the rules is when a woman doesn't know her value and what she can do. We tend to underestimate everything from our financial worth to our expertise, and therefore what opportunities might be available. Brenda Major, a social psychologist at the University of California at Santa Barbara, started studying the problem of self-perception decades ago. According to her research in 2014, it has been proven time and again that women will underestimate their performance, such as in exams and performance reviews, where men will typically overestimate. The women, of course, usually score way higher than they imagined when they are willing to participate.

When we discount our value, we are confined to the safe and familiar, and that continues to keep us playing small. As women, we must encourage one another to stretch and take relentless note of our worth. Telling her she is ready is part of that reminder. Moreover, there are also many opportunities that women cannot see and do not even know are available to them. Therefore, it's ever more important that we forge networks and alliances to be in support of one another. Jocelyn Mangan, from Him for Her, is a big advocate of telling women they are ready, especially in the context of women serving on boards. In our interview she told me, "I say put women in those opportunities sooner than they think they're ready. I spend most of my days telling board-ready women that they are actually board ready versus the alternative."

They are needed, according to National Public Radio's Lily Jamali, on March 5, 2020, "among the largest three thousand largest US publicly traded companies, only about one in five board members are women […] and nearly one in ten boards have no women at all." Jocelyn deeply believes, "what women can do for other women is encourage them that they're ready for that next thing, and if they can, putting them there too.

Even when that woman herself may not think she is quite ready." That would go a long way she told me. I think we can all agree.

There's a final piece I want to bring in about women and seeking permission to be ready. Neurobiologist and psychiatrist Louann Brizendine, of the University of California and author of *The Female Brain*, explains why there are many reasons behind this. From evolution that has the female brain more activated toward emotional response and, thus, seeking reassurance. To permission being reinforced as we grow up, with gender norms encouraging us as little girls to be still instead of curious, and later in the workplace being silenced and disliked when we do. It's a simple fact that we will seek out assurance, and one of the most powerful things you can do is help that woman give herself permission. She is the one who needs to give herself the green light, not us.

I think back to working mom, Erika Murdock Balbuena from Chapter 7, who decided to take her big role when a friend helped her think through all the possibilities. She did not give Erika permission, she helped her see she herself actually could do it and allowed her to know it was the right step for her. How liberating to give ourselves full permission to do, and be, all that we want and can be.

When we hear a wicked smart, accomplished, brilliant woman say she simply can't do it, it's gut wrenching. A part of you hurts deeply and you rush forward to help her up and motivate her along. The trouble is more often than not, we only hear that she didn't go for that big promotion, or the new job in a new state, or apply for that cool program until after the fact, when there was no way to support her decision. Telling her she is ready is therefore a continuous championing of proactively noticing, encouraging, and motivating her forward.

Marlow Blow, from Chapter 9 on "The Value of Investing," has a more specific take. She wants women to be ready because we need them to participate. "Our participation matters, and you should feel just as entitled to play in that game as everybody else and your male equivalent." Indeed, the more we show up, the more we play big, and the more we can do and be in the world. Being ready to take action is key, it's a virtuous circle where moving forward builds confidence, and that in turn creates more action.

So she got a new job offer? Tell her she is ready to negotiate a higher salary. She thinks it's not worth putting her hat in the ring for that big international project? Tell her she is ready and buoy her to try anyway. She doubts she has a chance? Tell her she is ready. We must keep pushing on. We are capable of more than we can imagine, and when we try, we see that's within the realm of all of us.

When we help another woman see that she is ready, we set a ripple effect in motion without end. Women are born ready. Sometimes we just need a gentle reminder to own our truth and claim our destiny.

CHAPTER 15

KEY #3—STAND BEHIND HER

———

When you do a Google search for "women standing behind women" almost every result returned is about a woman standing behind her man. You really have to search hard and only then will you find a handful of somewhat relevant returns. One bright spot I found was the beautiful Girl Scout annual campaign, "Stand Beside Her," which rallies "girls and women to stand up for each other, and [...] celebrate one another's talents and successes." But mostly one doesn't find a thing about how we as women stand behind our sisters.

That's clearly not a true indicator of how many women are supporting other women; however, I found it interesting there was hardly a mention using that turn of phrase. Just for a moment, imagine a world where at every turn, every woman knows—whether at home, at work, or anywhere else—there is always a group of women in full support of her, and they are willing to fight for her too.

If we want women stepping forward into the unknown and her full power then she needs to know, we

Stand Behind Her!

In writing this chapter, I took some time to think about the times I had taken a posture to stand behind a sister. Firstly, as a good friend it was easy to recall standing behind all of my dear friends' big decisions like moving back to China, getting married after doubting *he* actually was "the one," seeing a friend through a divorce, seeing another through their start-up failure, and championing many, many more to do the thing they thought they could never do. Standing behind her in these cases meant giving her what she needed to make a decision, backing her up to keep going, supporting her through struggles often tinged with regret, fear and shame, and holding her feet to the fire to push through to the other side.

Letting a girlfriend know I was there to talk, text, give advice, moral support, tough love, and copious amounts of caffeine was all part of being a damn good friend. That's what friends do, right? However, that can look very different in the workplace. When I contemplated the where and the how I had stood behind a woman at work, the examples were less than sparse.

I'm almost ashamed to admit I can hardly recall any significant moments, only a handful of times when I worked in large corporations where I lobbied for a team member's promotion, salary raises, and when I got behind key program initiatives led by women that would affect the entire organization. Once I was the person someone told about a sexual harassment incident, and I saw it through to the end. That doesn't seem much when I look back at a twenty-five-year career.

In talking with many of the women I interviewed, this is a consistent theme throughout a large amount of their careers. Although now so many of us are passionately outspoken in support of women and have founded organizations actively working to create systemic change. In a typical corporation, though, it's understandably harder to help at work where not "rocking the boat" rules supreme. Further, it turns out there is a proven disincentive to helping. According to Jessica Bennet for *Inc Magazine*, a 2016 study published in the *Academy of Management Journal* found that senior-level women who try to help other women at work are likely to face more negative performance reviews than those who don›t. So it's already hard to help, and when we do, we pay for it.

Noticing and supporting your sisters at work though, can be done in many ways. Emotional support is an easy lift and can be key to helping a work colleague do what she wants and needs to do. Karen Kimsey-House, who is cofounder of The Co-Active Training Institute and also sits on my board of directors at The Coaching Fellowship, writes and teaches extensively about leadership and has always encouraged me in my work to lead generously through relationship. When I reflected on my own personal standing behind another woman, I had actually discounted the hundreds, perhaps thousands of moments in the office where I provided a kind word, extra time, and yes, in some cases a hug. The number of times I did are endless—supporting a woman after a boss chewed her out, deconstructing a bad annual review, consoling her after a significant request that was denied. There was no end to the number of times I walked around the block, got a Starbucks, and texted well into the night. But was that enough to really help?

In Karen's book *Co-Active Leadership: Five Ways to Lead,* she writes, "when someone is walking beside us, we have more courage to walk into the unknown and to risk the dark and messy places in our journey." As women, we do this so naturally and beautifully for our friends and can see the generative results. By extending the same sense of sisterhood at work, we can bring untold benefits to increase our colleagues' self-worth, solidify their decisions, and have them coming back stronger again and again. In fact, according to research cited in *Business Wire* in 2020, women are 2.5 times more likely to become high performers if they have a tight-knit circle of supportive women at work.

When I think back to how I helped back then, I gave out copious positive acknowledgments, tried to help the person see the whole picture, and set them up to come back tomorrow and try again. Funny, now years later, it's hard not to see those women as victims of some of the biggest gender bias offenses—receiving negative personal feedback, being passed over for top level opportunities, and being talked over and silenced. So, let's be clear, not everyone at work is someone you want to be best friends with, maybe not even friends with at all, but there is a way for us to extend our gifts to help that woman succeed, which works to combat bias and will help all of us succeed.

That brings me to my next point, where there is always a discussion about how women do not help other women in the workplace. Dubbed as the "sisterhood ceiling" by PepsiCo CEO Indra Nooyi, while speaking at *The New York Times* Women in the World Summit, Monty Majeed reported for Herstory, Nooyi said, "I don't believe women help women enough in the workplace [...] what's wrong with us women? We ought to be helping each other out." Personally, I have never found that to be true, but as the big idea for my book explains, I think women could help women more often, and when they do the flywheel I speak of, it often gets kicked up a gear.

More often than not, as cited by Anne Welsh McNulty in *The Harvard Business Review* in 2018, there are so few women at the top that women feel they have to act like men, consciously distancing themselves from junior women in the workplace, and thus provide them no support at all. By contrast, "men are 46 percent more likely to have a higher-ranking advocate in the office." Then there's the so-called "Queen Bee Syndrome," documented by Shawn Andrews in his 2018 book, *The Power of Perception*, where women display a toughness, which keeps us from standing behind our female colleagues as they try to rise in the ranks.

While there is evidence this is all true, what is also apparent is the shift that's been quietly happening for more than a decade. The tipping point is often attributed to former Secretary of State Madeleine Albright, when in her keynote address documented by *USA Today* at the Celebrating Inspiration luncheon she said, "there is a special place in hell for women who don't help other women." Shawn Andrews goes on to write the saying has been "repeated by hundreds of women around the world, including heads of state and celebrities, and shows the collective shift in mindset by many women." In my interviews, I must have heard it dozens of times, so it still rings true.

There's even more reason to help support women, and more women taking on positions of leadership. In 2018, Pew research reported by Kim Parker, has found that the higher percentage of women in the workplace, the lower the levels of gender discrimination and bias. One cannot help but see the flywheel in action again. The more empowered women we have, the more there will be. By helping another, we ultimately help ourselves in the process.

Finally, there are times when standing behind her means taking a risk and a strong stand for what's right. Whether we see a woman being talked over, being disrespected behind her back, or being the object of a clear abuse of power, privilege, and position, it is our responsibility to speak and act. Fighting for something and someone we believe in is paramount to change.

Some days a kind word will go a long way. On others, let's be ready to speak up, defend, call out, and call forward. We must be impatient for our sisters to thrive. When you stand behind her, remember you are taking an active stand for all women. You are taking progress into your own hands.

CHAPTER 16

KEY #4—HELP HER HELP HERSELF

———

We are all searching for the right answers. We want all the advice to assess the options and risk. We want all the reassurance that what we choose is tested and true. We want all the experts and all the experience on board. When the going gets hard, most of us would feel a lot better if someone would simply tell us what to do. But you know as well as me, that's not how it works. As tough as it seems, to truly own our lives, empower ourselves, and others, we must make our own decisions. When we do, our commitment deepens, the likelihood of success expands, and the potential for deep fulfillment increases.

We live in a world where women feel we must be perfect, says Jessica Bennett, in a *TIME* article from 2014 on how perfectionism holds women back. Research from My Confidence Matters in association with the University of Glasgow in 2017, has found more than 73 percent of women lacked confidence at work on a regular basis. Furthermore, as women, we are wired to help where we believe we have an obligation to offer our support, and we will rush forward at any given moment. But one of the most powerful, supportive, and empowering acts you can do to help a sister succeed is to,

Help Her Help Herself!

This is a deeply meaningful lesson I learned when I trained to become a coach at The Co-Active Training Institute. Helping someone help themselves is a fundamental principle of coaching. A coach will not share their advice, experience, or opinion, rather, their role is to help that person see everything that's available to them for them to clearly make the best choice. This way of being has since become one of my core values in life and is, in my opinion, a critically important, different, and liberating way of supporting a sister.

Before becoming a coach, I had always considered myself the "helper." Given an opportunity, I was delighted to be in support of another human being. It was how I was raised and what I believed constituted the core of being a good person. But I learned helping can sometimes cause more harm than good. It can backfire, people end up not following through, and arguments and blame can follow. And worse, our help can crucially take away another person's power and potential.

According to a 2017 article by Sarah A. Benton in *Psychology Today,* helping "does not allow the other individual to take responsibility for her own actions and to develop internal motivation." When we rush to help another, they may not learn the vital skills of self-sufficiency or even believe they are themselves capable of success. Helping can be the very opposite of what we imagine.

It's normal to want to help. *Scientific American* explained in 2012, we have evolved over millennia by cooperating to survive and thrive, but our desire to want to be in service in modern day times can also be detrimental to ourselves. The so-called "Savior Complex" is a condition whereby we feel compelled to "save" others and may sacrifice our own needs over theirs further describes Benton's article in *Psychology Today*. Furthermore, the simple weight of holding another's problems as well as our own can be an immense and over-whelming load to carry. Helping a sister help herself, there-fore, is a deeply empowering act and one that allows you to give your full self without losing you.

Of course, you do not need to be a trained coach to help another person. Many of us are natural coaches. Take being a parent for an example. Consider how you help your children learn and grow. It's usually through a brief teaching moment, then a lot of coaching them to do it all on their own. Kids love exploring, choosing, and taking action—who would they grow up to be if we didn't let them help themselves? As adults, later in life it is no different, so changing how we give is so essential. Help a woman see that she has all she needs inside her to move forward and encourage her to seek out sounding boards, rather than helpers. This coaching approach breeds self-assurance and self-respect.

This important stance came up time and again in my inter-views for this book. Kathryn Minshew, founder of The Muse, in particular, was a passionate advocate for not diving in head first with giving advice. She told me the most impactful thing you can do to support another woman is "to listen intently, and get her to trust her own gut and instincts, because I think we know the best answers for ourselves." Kathryn reflected herself on the number of times people had told her what they thought she should do, but she says the trouble is "you rarely truly know what someone should or shouldn't do unless you're sitting in their seat."

Kathryn went on to explain how as she built her business serving more than seventy-five million customers "people would continually share what they did, and why it worked, or why it backfired, and that was all very valuable information," she says. However, Kathryn found those who were most helpful to her had "listened, and asked thoughtful questions that helped me better understand the problem. The calls that really sting are the ones where I knew better. I knew in my gut, and I didn't do it because I let somebody else talk me into something different." When it came to the people who most supported Kathryn, it was always those who said to her "only you know what can make this decision right."

What Kathryn is pointing out is the fine line between mentoring and coaching, and we need both. Mentoring helps by sharing your expertise and drawing advice from likely decades of experiences. We all love to share what we've learned, and we sincerely don't want people to make the same mistakes we did. The catch though, is that at the end of the day, the person still needs to make that important decision for herself. A former boss of mine, John Lilly, former CEO of Mozilla would often say "there are maps, they are just not your maps." This is so true. So encourage her to consult the maps, including yours, but make sure she charts her own course too.

Liz Jenkins, chief operating officer at Hello Sunshine, founded by Reese Witherspoon, also shared with me that we should "listen first, and not assume what works for you will work for her." She told me a story from last summer, when a Black female associate who was having a challenge in her own workplace asked Liz for support. "It was interesting because I recognized I had to hold myself back from saying to her she should do what I did. I love jumping in and helping, but I've had to learn to smile, and let it kind of roll off of me. I remember, in the moment, it being really hard for me to not say well this is what you should do. It's so critical not to be directive, now I like to tell stories to get to the bottom of what are you thinking about and what are you struggling with." Liz knew it was good to share her own experience, but it was more important to help the person find the answer for themselves. Asking better questions will help that person get to better answers.

I think we can all agree we know ourselves better than anyone, but sometimes we need some help to see and believe that this is true. Karen Kimsey-House, cofounder of The Co-Active Training Institute, codeveloped their coaching philosophy around a key tenant being to hold someone "naturally, creative, resourceful, and whole." It means to hold a fundamental belief that people have deep within them a source of knowledge and strength. They already have all they need to succeed and move forward. They are not broken and don't need fixing or saving. It's merely our jobs to help them see this for themselves. I find this a noble perspective, one where our help is additive for another person's growth on both an external and internal level.

So help her help herself because when she does, she is more likely to go the extra mile, she will truly (and finally) believe she is as powerful as she really is, she will go forward and help others find their answers, and she will bring us all with her.

CHAPTER 17

KEY #5—ACTUALLY TALK ABOUT MONEY

———

With greater economic security and empowerment, there are no limits to what we as women can accomplish. With increased wealth, we increase independence, self-sufficiency, and opportunity for ourselves and our families. With increased wealth, we invest in ways that can make positive change and a return. With an increase in wealth, we increase our power to decide and choose what is important and most needed in the world.

But our relationship with money is complicated and awkward. It's one of the last big taboos for women. We've been conditioned since the dawn of capitalism that the men take care of the money. They have been taught to grow it and pursue it, we have been taught to save it, and be careful with it. However, if we don't talk about money, we can't build a positive relationship with it, we can't put it to use, and we all remain separated in our experience and learning. That's why it's critical for women to connect, and

Actually Talk about Money

Sally Krawcheck is CEO and cofounder of Ellevest, the first financial company built by women, specifically for women to reach $1 billion in client investments, as reported by Jessica Thomas for *Entrepreneur,* in March 2021. Admired for her outspoken views, she is often quoted as saying women would rather discuss what they did in the bedroom last night than talk about money. In one article, she penned for the Ellevest blog in 2018, she said, "You know a subject's really taboo when people would rather talk about their weight, discuss politics and religion, sit down for 'the birds and the bees,' or ask an adult child to move out."

Money really is the last untouchable conversation. A 2015 study from Fidelity Investments reported, "four in five women have, at some point, refrained from talking about their finances to those they are close with." The most common reasons that hold women back from talking money with loved ones are it's too personal and too awkward a subject, it's something they were brought up not to talk about, and it doesn't seem like the kind of information you should share.

But if we don't talk about money, we are not going to be able to increase our familiarity and, therefore, our expertise. And that will stop us from increasing not only our own wealth, but the wealth of those around us too. It's a subject that we further punish ourselves badly for not understanding.

Kristin Hull, CEO of Nia Impact Capital, painted a vivid picture of this in my interview with her, "I don't know how to build a skyscraper, I never studied it, and it does not keep me up at night. Likewise, I knew nothing about heart surgery, I didn't study that either. I trust the people who did and are doing their jobs. But why is that different with women and finance? We didn't study it, no one talked to us about it, why should we know how to do it? And, then, why would we feel shame about something we were never taught?" That's where we come in and initiate. Talking about money is only awkward because we don't talk about it enough. And when we do, women act.

When we engage in a conversation about money, we increase the likelihood that another woman might ask for help about money across the board. If she sees we have a financial advisor, she might be more likely to find one for herself. If she learns we have made investments, it might pique her interest. If she hears about the women-owned businesses we have supported and increased our return on investment, maybe she will have a go herself. I love to imagine a world where we might share trading tips as well as that no-knead dough recipe. We love to share, so if we could just make a start, there's a massive groundswell of knowledge and willingness to help sitting under our noses.

Even worse for women than talking about money in general, is talking about how much we earn. The gender pay gap is real and closing at a glacial pace. We are still decades away from equal pay for white women. As Sally Krawcheck for *Ellevest Magazine* in 2019 sadly explains, we are also "one hundred-plus years away for equal pay for Black women, and two hundred-plus years for Latina women." Perhaps, one of the biggest hurdles we can help overcome is supporting women in asking for what they are worth. When we share our own salaries and discuss strategies for asking for a raise, we increase the likelihood of her claiming what she is owed.

However, regardless of our personal relationship with money, there are systemic money challenges for women. As Sally Krawcheck said, "women face the pink tax, the wage gap, the debt gap, the funding gap, the domestic work (and emotional labor) gap, and—her personal crusade—the investing gap." It's hard to know where to tackle such deep rooted and widespread problems.

There is might in numbers and collective action though, and that's where there's power when a group of women comes together to support each other with the financial conversations they need to have. For example, it's great to see a growing number of investor circle organizations out there such as Invest for Better, which is designed to help women invest. It's also possible to start closer to home and create your own money conversation circle with a handful of women in your network like Sophie McNaught originally did. They do not have to be intimidating affairs. It could be meeting at a friend's house, or on Zoom with five to ten others once a month to share doubts, fears, experiences, what investments you are doing, and ideas for moving your money forward. As women, we deeply know how to connect and help each other forward, and now we need to do that with our money conversations too.

Other lightweight lifts might include sharing money-focused books, articles, podcasts, and other resources. Being the example is an equally important manifestation. When you talk about money, share about money, and naturally bring this conversation into the spotlight, you are demonstrating it's okay to do so and dispelling many money myths.

And, if you needed any other motivation to help another woman, just listen to Sophie McNaught again. She told me one of her biggest fears would be if one of the women she loves and cares about ended up in a precarious financial situation just because she didn't know some simple things about money that she should have. We've all seen our friends get divorced, lose a job, and hopefully they have been able to come through. But what happens if they have a period of extended illness, there's an accident, or something else unexpected happens that needed their finances to already be in order?

No one wants financial hardship to happen, but if it does and we are not prepared, that's a tragedy that might have been avoided. Sophie explained, "that's where I feel my obligation. No one I know is going to turn around and say, 'I just had no idea other people were doing these things, no one told me.'" Moreover, even beyond unforeseen events, today women live longer than men by six to eight years, but we retire with two thirds of the amount of money as men, reported Akshita Gandra for *Business Journal* in 2019. I think of my aging widowed mum and the heartbreaking statistic shared by Monique Morrissey from the Economic Policy Institute 2019 Economic Snapshot, which states that regardless of race, education, and marital status, women sixty-five and over are 80 percent more likely to live in poverty than men. This is something we have to change by helping each other learn and talk about our finances and maximize our hard-earned wealth.

In 2021, women—at least in the Western world—have access to financial information, legal rights, opportunities to work, and are able to participate economically. What were once barriers are not barriers any more. What we need is sweeping cultural change where women are excited by, outspoken for, and perfectly comfortable with money. For that to happen, we need to talk about it every single day. We need to make it as normal as dropping our kids off at school or making a grocery list.

As feminist icon, Gloria Steinem, was quoted as saying by T. Shawn Taylor for the *Chicago Tribune* back in 2003, "We'll never solve the feminization of power until we solve the masculinity of wealth." We can do that by empowering the women around us to have a female relationship with money. One that is nurturing, transparent, where it's put to the uses we care about, and where it serves a meaningful purpose.

Talking about money is squarely about creating financial security, but it's also about how we want the rest of the world to look. The people who have control of capital are able to decide what has value and what problems are worth solving. Women need to be part of that conversation, and we can help us get there.

CHAPTER 18

KEY #6—STAND UP FOR HER

———

Of all the ten keys to unlocking an empowered woman, this one may require the most courage. Taking a stand is the moment when we feel compelled to act on our values and convictions, even if it means taking a substantial risk. Think of Rosa Parks who, in the face of entrenched segregation, chose to sit down on the bus on her way home from work at the department store. Taking a stand is a bold act. It means acting in support of what you care most deeply about.

As empowered women, there will be times when taking a stand for our sisters is the only choice left to make. We can help another woman help herself. We can create potential opportunities for growth. We can share our wisdom and advice, but there will come a time when the only thing left to do is

Stand Up for Her!

When I interviewed Rachel Thomas, the cofounder and CEO of LeanIn.org, she shared her single best advice to help another woman was to take a stand. "I want women to realize that when you advocate for other women, it's actually good for you too. It elevates your status and presents you more as more of a leader." Rachel is a firm believer in women taking a stand for each other. She went on, "My biggest thing is that women should wake up every morning and think I'm going to be the boldest, loudest, proudest ally for other women. Then do it unapologetically and often." I couldn't agree more.

Standing up for her might be by confronting senior management of the need to improve your organization's diversity, it might be by reporting bias against working mothers passed over for opportunities and advancement, it might be by advocating for a female hire, or by directly challenging a colleague who made a gendered joke. It might also look like calling on other women in a meeting for their opinion, crediting a female colleague for her idea, or asking a male colleague to get coffee for guests or take notes instead of the young woman who always volunteers to help.

Standing up for her means doing so in big and small ways, but it requires our willingness to take action and to also potentially face the consequences. This key comes with publicly expressing your opinion, often in a work setting, on stage while giving a speech, in an interview, or posting to social media. That action could create everything from a raised eyebrow, to trolling on your Twitter feed, to conflict, criticism, ridicule, and professional blow back. Taking a stand comes with risks, and that's something we all need to weigh as we decide which course of action to take.

But when we feel compelled to act, it sometimes comes out of nowhere, and there isn't much time to think, only do. A few years ago, I was invited, at the last minute, to attend a Red Bull event. I jumped at the chance, as it was sure to be filled with creative people along with inspiring talks on innovative ideas and projects. After ninety minutes, it dawned on me that I hadn't yet seen a woman on stage, and when I looked more closely at the agenda, there was only going to be one token woman almost at the close. I felt my face flush with rage, then shame for being there, and then the compulsion came. It rose up out of me, and I simply had to put it somewhere. I got out of my seat and rushed to find the organizer to let him know what I thought. I was calm but firm, and I told him I would never have said yes to attending if I knew this was the lineup. He agreed with me and admitted it was more than an oversight to have such few women experts.

What he did next was admirable. There was a thirty-minute open mic segment to start the sessions after lunch, where anyone from the audience could speak for five minutes on a topic of their choice. He asked me to speak first and address what I had told him privately, publicly. I was terrified and of course said yes. I spoke as eloquently as I could about the importance of representation, on making sure all voices and perspectives are heard, and that it was 2017, God damn it! When my time was up, I was greeted with a standing ovation. And then, it was deemed (by the audience I might add) that every other open mic speaker that day should be a woman.

My small act took my own breath away and made an impact I didn't expect. As I stepped off the stage, still shaking a little, several women and men came up to me to thank me for bringing everyone's attention to the lack of women's perspectives being presented on stage. I realized then how important it is to follow the urge to stand up for what I believe in, not only to satisfy my own need to act in alignment with my values, but because I am also most likely representing others when I do so.

When we let our values and beliefs guide us, we are compelled to take action to support fairness, equality, and truth, especially when we see those principles being violated. Standing up for her becomes the only right thing to do.

Think back to the story of Tracy Chou, who took a small bold step to call on technology companies to release their diversity numbers, and forever changed the face of Silicon Valley. Her simple blog post and call to action drove a critical turning point for data-driven people to finally "see" the appalling numbers for women in technology with hard evidence. Years later, being interviewed by Elaine Burke at Silicon Republic in 2017, Tracy described the struggle of women and minorities as, "death by a thousand paper cuts" and added that "countering those thousand paper cuts means lots and lots of little interventions." At the time, Tracy hadn't considered her efforts an activist endeavor, but she took a stand, and that led her to becoming a global champion for gender equality.

Lots of little interventions is the backdrop of how we all can stand up for her, whose total sum might just create a landslide of change. One of the small such acts multiplied by the hundreds is ensuring women are heard. The statistics for women being talked over and silenced, even at the highest levels of power, are devastatingly high. Political scientist research from Adam Grant for *The Washington Post* in 2021, shows that when groups of five make democratic decisions, if only one member is a woman, she will speak 40 percent less than the men. The study goes on to say, "only in groups with four women do they finally take up as much airtime as men."

Furthermore, there are still many critical institutions where women have no ability to speak at all. Take the recent February 2021 scandal reported by The Guardian's Justin McCurry, of the "Liberal Democratic Party, which has governed Japan almost unchallenged since 1955. It had proposed allowing groups of about five women to attend meetings of its twelve-member board, ten of whom are men, on condition they remained silent observers." It reads like an article you might have seen in 1950. But, even when we hold positions of power and influence and we have permission to actually speak, women being heard is still not guaranteed. In the workplace, that's an easy stand for us to take and do every day to magnify and legitimize another woman's voice.

Amplification was an approach that women in the White House devised, explained Juliet Eilperin for *The Washington Post* in 2016, when even though they reached parity in numbers with their male colleagues under President Obama, they were still continually having to fight to be heard and have their expertise valued. They came up with a plan to amplify each other, so whereby when a woman in a White House meeting made a contribution, shared an idea, or gave her opinion, another woman seated at the table would repeat it. This made the point undeniable, giving her legitimacy and not giving the men in the room the chance to either deny her or claim the idea as their own.

One thing is true, it is more compelling to stand *for* something than against it, maybe not as easy, but it is more powerful. Demonstrating our support for another woman has movement and forward momentum, and it's a way we are working to create something better. But when we are against something, we are only addressing the symptoms of the problem and there is resistance and confrontation. Rather than being against the patriarchy, we can be for women's advancement. Rather than being against men talking so much, we can be for women speaking more. Standing for something is active and even celebratory. Think of jumping to your feet when a goal is scored or giving a standing ovation to a performance that moved you. Standing up for her shows your appreciation as well as working to solve the underlying problems she is experiencing.

So let's call upon each other for ideas, speak up when we see a sister trying desperately to say something, call out interruptions from your male colleagues, repeat good advice, and reinforce expertise and opinions. Every day, we are surrounded by moments when we can take a positive stand for another woman, so let's jump to our feet and get moving!

CHAPTER 19

KEY #7—BE THE EXAMPLE

—

When we think of role models, we initially tend to think of influential, famous, and enduring figures such as Ruth Bader Ginsburg, Beyoncé, or Malala Yousafzai. They are women who captivated our attention, have often been celebrated for being the first, and have generated a tremendous amount of impact in the world. As women in prominent roles, they are critical for showing us that the highest echelons of power and influence are possible and within reach for all of us.

We also need to have role models closer to home. Women we see at work, in our communities, in our families, and in our places of worship. These are the role models who inspire us, motivate us, and show us what's truly possible. That's where you come in.

Whether we are aware of it or not, our actions and examples are constantly being observed. Without knowing it, we might have already inspired another to take a leap of faith. When we consciously share our stories and successes, we increase the likelihood of more being heard. So for more women to see the possibilities, see how it's done, and see that they too can do it, we need you to

Be the Example!

With so few women in positions of power and influence, it is critical to create more role models for women and girls so that they might imagine a future for themselves where they can achieve their dreams and reach their fullest potential.

When they can imagine themselves walking the same path as their role models, they are encouraged to reach higher, push further, and try a little harder. When someone's efforts, words, and deeds touch them deeply, they are more willing to reach outside of their comfort zone and try to follow in the wake of another woman who has forged the way.

For me, it began with my grandmother, whose grace modeled strength with serenity. Then figures like dot-com champion Martha Lane Fox, who cofounded Lastminute.com in 1998. She was pushing the edges of what was possible in business when I was beginning my career. I was never starstruck by actresses and pop stars. My heroines looked more like Jane Goodall and the peace-broker, Mo Mowlam. Later, women role models who I worked closely with were the ones who motivated me to be and do more, such as Mitchell Baker, Athena Katsaros, and Karen Kimsey-House. And today, the hundreds of young women social change makers I support through my work at The Coaching Fellowship keep me going and inspire my life's work.

At the end of 2020, we witnessed a significant role model breaking onto the national and international stage when Kamala Harris became the first woman, and the first woman of color, in the US to be elected vice president. In her acceptance speech, as reported by Lauren Gambino for The Guardian in November 2020, she made a promise, "While I may be the first woman in this office. I will not be the last because every little girl watching tonight sees that this is a country of possibilities." Even though we have made massive and vastly important strides forward, women occupy only 0.5 percent of history books, according to Jessica Bennett, of *The New York Times,* in 2019. It's clear we need more women in view, and we need to rewrite the history that actually happened.

Few women have held influential positions, and with those who did being written out of history, is it any wonder that the broad majority of our examples of success are inherently male? Across leadership in business, science, education, government, the arts, and more, our lack of female role models impacts how we see what's possible for ourselves and our sisters. As Dr. Nina Ansary, UN Women Global Champion and author of *Anonymous Is a Woman*, said in a 2019 interview with Poultney Carducci for World News Era, "Raising the visibility of women in *every* sphere of endeavor is vital to empowering women and achieving gender parity. It takes an accumulation of role models—real life examples of what girls and women can do if given the opportunity—to change entrenched attitudes."

Having a multitude of positive examples of smart, powerful women creating change and living bold and authentic lives is key to empowering another woman. And yes, I am talking about you being that example.

One of our big challenges as women is that we find it hard to see ourselves as role models. We think we need to have achieved a particular position or level of accomplishment before we have something to say and offer. And even when we have attained that hallowed standing, we are less likely to brag about our achievements, and we are more likely to discount our success and be hesitant in sharing our story.

Perhaps, it's also because our own lack of role models means it doesn't come easy to imagine we too might be a lighthouse for another woman to see. One of my mentors, Mitchell Baker, cofounder of Mozilla, told me many times that she never had any role models. At the same time, she struggled with being seen as a female icon in technology, even though she has inspired thousands of women to study and lead in technology. An October 2020 article Margie Warrell wrote for *Forbes* on female roles summed it up perfectly, she said, "I encourage you to be the role model you wished you'd had when you were starting out."

Role models do many things and take many forms. They inspire and motivate us, they also demonstrate how to be in the world, and how to make things happen. Think of women in your life who have overcome obstacles, who kept going, and who created success on their own terms. These are inspiring women who show us every day the possible ways to move forward and actualize our potential. These are similarly your struggles and challenges, and when you share how you are coping and finding ways forward, others will follow.

Katya Libin, CEO and cofounder of HeyMama, agrees and thinks vulnerability is such a powerful tool. In our interview, she explained "we're so filled with images of perfection. You might see someone on Instagram and it looks like they have it completely together, but no one knows they had an epic fail that day." We discussed how misguiding that can be because we're all dealing with pain and struggle, and yet, Katya went on, "When we share an experience that someone else could relate to, it might open them up as well. Being vulnerable is so powerful for ourselves as well as others." Just as Katya was telling me this, I could hear her little one crying loudly in the background, and I remarked how perfect timing that was. "Yes, you know, this is life. And, you know, and that's totally fine."

Another aspect of sharing your story is to demystify how you actually got there. The answer is always with a lot of hard work, but success can look daunting and impossible if you are standing on the outside. I've been told my background and work history can look a little intimidating. When that happens, I am always quick to share that I was the first kid in my family with a college degree, both my parents worked in factories their whole lives, and the first three years of my working life I too spent working in a factory. I credit my experience there to truly teaching me the power of relationships and hard work. Again, demystifying who you are and how you got here are powerful stories that help another woman see they might too be able to do it for themselves.

Of course, we need more than role models to aspire to. We need systemic change to create gender parity within our organizations and institutions. Colonel Candice Frost was not only the US Army glass ceiling breaker, but she went on and still does loudly advocate for change within the military. We must highlight and amplify the work of women creators and leaders just like Liz Jenkins is doing at Hello Sunshine. We must make sure every woman and girl can imagine the different lives they might live, the different jobs they might do, and the different outcomes they might influence. And that it's their right to do so.

Being the example means we are living our full beautiful imperfect lives, where others can see our truth, our power, and our wisdom. Let's shine our lights brightly so we know we can set the world on fire.

CHAPTER 20

KEY #8—GIVE HER CONFIDENCE

———

"We are what we think. All that we are, arises with our thoughts. With our thoughts, we make the world," so Buddha said. Our thoughts and beliefs and therefore our actions, shape our lives every day and ultimately determine our future.

When I think about writing this book, there were moments when I truly struggled. I told myself I wasn't smart enough and almost gave up. A dear friend often helped me reframe my perspective and reconnect with why I decided to write it in the first place. She helped me see I was doubling my suffering by adding extra weight of my own making to something that was already a hugely involved project. Helping me see why I was the person to write about empowering women gave me confidence and connection to carry on. The result is in your hands.

The mind has the power to build ourselves up or tear ourselves down, and with the weight of a single thought, greatness or folly can be decided.

When we have confidence, we trust in ourselves, our abilities, and our potential. We are willing to take risks, try again, and push harder. When we have confidence, we have a deep faith that we are on the right track, and we know regardless of what happens we will figure it out. But that can change quickly with a negative experience, an opportunity denied, and not being seen or heard. When our inner voice starts the cacophony of worthlessness, it's hard to feel emboldened and brave enough to carry on.

Confidence is built in unison when we believe in us and when others believe in us, too. Individually, we can doubt and struggle and fear, but together we can be stronger, more resilient, and bigger than the sum of the parts. We can all grow in size, courage, and significance when we

Give Her Confidence!

Regardless of our age and achievements, confidence is not a full-blown conclusion. Just because we made it to the next level doesn't mean we still don't have concerns. In fact, being successful can increase our self-doubt and beliefs that we don't own the right to be there. A 2020 KPMG study found that 75 percent of female executives across a multitude of industries have experienced imposter syndrome and nearly half of those women said that their self-doubt was as a result from never expecting to reach the level of success they have achieved. With so few women who have reached a position of power, it's not difficult to believe. Katty Kay, author of the 2014 book, *The Confidence Code,* says in a *TIME Magazine* article from the same year it's, "important for women to recognize that it's totally normal for us to feel nervous, particularly in situations in which we're so often the only woman in the room."

Lack of confidence is something that we all experience at one point or another, so when you look around, you can be certain it is not only the younger women in our midst but also our peers and definitely those we look up to as well. Self-doubt is debilitating, whether it stops us from speaking up in a meeting, or going for that big promotion, or asking for what we are worth. It's a big problem, but thankfully with some support and coaching, confidence is something that can be increased and have the women in our lives bringing their complete selves to the table.

The KMPG study further shows that women who feel valued and acknowledged in their work and have mentors and advisors to guide them, are less likely to experience imposter syndrome. When we feel truly seen and appreciated, then our self-worth increases and we have a strong foundation to grow our confidence. As empowered women, this is a great place for us to start and an easy lift. Let's make sure we are available for the women around us and be sure to generously point out their successes and strengths.

The deep building of confidence, however, is to encourage her to step outside of her comfort zone. Low confidence breeds low confidence. People who are unwilling to take on new and unfamiliar challenges find themselves in a race to the bottom, whereas those with higher self-esteem have more successes and, thus, more confidence to take on challenges beyond their safe place.

Confidence and action are a virtuous circle. When we believe we will be successful, we take action and we move forward. When we move forward, the belief in ourselves and our abilities increases, and we gain more confidence to take another action, and so on.

So our role becomes to encourage her to take a step in this cycle. If she is doubting her abilities, help her see her strengths and previous successes. If she is struggling to take a first step, help her move past her hesitation. When we demonstrate a deep sense of trust in her, we help increase her self-esteem and activate an inner strength and fortitude.

Toni Maloney, the cofounder of Bpeace also thinks, "the biggest thing a woman of presence of power and achievement can do for another woman is to give her legitimate confidence. Not just a 'oh you're so great,' not superficial confidence, but genuine deep dive confidence." In our interview, Toni shared it's critical to articulate often to the women around you that they are doing an incredibly good job or call out what traits are serving them well. Toni told me about a new young woman Bpeace had just hired. "You can see her day by day growing in confidence because of the feedback she's getting from her supervisor. How wonderful to build somebody up, rather than tearing someone down." How wonderful indeed.

Giving confidence and praise is something we can each do every day, and with your appreciation and celebration, you might just give her the boost she needs. When a female colleague does something out of her comfort zone, take the time to acknowledge not only what she did, but the courage it took to do it. Deep-dive confidence building means pointing out the character qualities someone has that make them unique and help them move forward in their lives and careers. Qualities might include taking a risk that others weren't willing to take, being willing to say something in a meeting that needed to be said, having integrity in the face of a challenge, or listening with compassion to a coworker. You can also let her know the positive impact she has on you and others around her. The key is to say what you genuinely see and feel. This is not about complimenting someone to be nice, not at all. It's about holding a positive mirror up to other women so they can clearly see what their positive qualities and impacts are.

Imagine the women in your life walking away from your conversation with a spring in their step! And you can too. In a March 2018 *Inc. Magazine* article, Wanda Thibodeaux explained how complimenting someone can increase your long-term positive thinking, up your courage, and encourage quick adaptation and decision-making.

I love the idea of empowering people so much that they will surprise you and that they are capable of exceeding your expectations, their own and everyone around them. If people are given fertile ground on which to build and create, they will time and again over-deliver, grow exponentially, and raise the stakes for all of us.

One of my all-time favorite stories to share is writer and lecturer Joseph Campbell's *The Hero's Journey*, which was first released as a book in 1990. I like to call it, the "Heroine's Journey." If you aren't familiar with this tale, our hero or heroine is the basis for every great novel, movie, and story ever told. It goes like this, our protagonist is moving about their lives, then one day, they hear "the call" to embark on a great quest. Along the way they go on many journeys and encounter many obstacles, including one big one that ultimately lands them in the pit, the darkest and lowest point of their adventure. This is the most critical and arduous point, and it's actually also the most gripping part for us, the viewer, as we sit on the edge of our seats. We are enthralled by their struggles, wondering if they will make it, and captivated by their eventual triumph.

As every great story demonstrates, the two things that help our heroine escape from the pit and fulfill her purpose are faith and allies. Faith in the process, herself, her skills, and mission. And allies, the people around her to help lift her up, out, and onward. As empowered women, we can do both to help a sister advance and get her on her way. We can believe in her, show her she is capable, and celebrate her success, and we can be her ally in reaching out our hands to pull her forward. Confidence requires we trust in ourselves and that we are seen and witnessed by others who also believe in us.

But when the going gets really tough, and someone has lost their faith and reminding them of their abilities is not enough, it often helps to reorientate people to their value, mission, and purpose. Personally, I know where I have found the most strength in myself was when I deeply believed in what I was trying to achieve and that my efforts were worthwhile. I know I am motivated by democratizing access, by enabling others, and working to creating a culture and society based on mutual support and empowerment. When I can align my values and purpose with my work, then my confidence soars,

I am more willing to risk, put myself out there and push to get as far as I can. By helping her see what she is here to do, you can unlock a deep well of strength and fortitude.

Sometimes a lack of confidence arises from doing work that is not fully aligned with our values and aspirations. When I look back at my early career, I can see that I was in love with the idea of some roles. A big marketing career, for example, but the reality of those roles left me dissatisfied and exhausted. I only began to thrive when my work was congruent with my strengths and values. Sometimes that meant choosing a position that had less prestige or where I earned less money. But the fulfillment I felt gave me boundless energy and my confidence grew as I followed my desire to bring my whole self to the world. So when you speak to another woman who is doubting herself, make sure you also listen for dissonance in her current situation and help her see what she really wants to do.

In my work with The Coaching Fellowship, the vast majority of the highly successful and impactful young women we work with want to spend their time with their coach working on increasing their confidence. When I first started my organization, this fact would upset me greatly. These social change leaders were highly accomplished, using their talents to create a better world, and yet their lack of confidence stood in the way of them unlocking even more of their potential. This repeating theme disheartened me until I realized that our coaches had the exact set of skills needed to address it. Through coaching, each of our fellows have the opportunity to build their confidence as they cultivate their leadership. It is in the relationship with a coach who can reflect back to her who she is that these young, powerful women learn to trust in themselves and their unique gifts.

Building her self-assurance, supporting her next big step, and celebrating her achievements are all within our reach to empower a woman forward. Confidence is a real issue, but when she is surrounded by a group of strong, encouraging women, we can help her shine brightly, and live her full potential.

CHAPTER 21

KEY #9—SEND THE ELEVATOR DOWN

———

When we are standing on top of a mountain and can look down to see how far we've come, I hope it's with an overwhelming sense of pride and deep achievement. Because for women to make it to the top on their own terms, and not by trying to mimic their male colleagues, it's not only a clear indication of sheer hard work but also a mark of pure grit and determination for what was needed to carve out our own untrodden and upward path. Take Lindsay Kaplan, cofounder at Chief.com from Chapter 2 on women and networking, who not only leads authentically and publicly as a mother, but strives daily with her company to support women ascending their own mountains. Or Sophie McNaught from Chapter 10 on women and investing, who in her spare time helps women become comfortable talking about money and teaches them how to invest. Whether directly or indirectly, they are creating ways to help more women advance.

For many of us, there was no one to help us rise. There was no Sherpa, no compass and no map, just our absolute tenacity, self-belief, and resilience to get as far as we have. At times, it's been as exhausting as the long, slow, altitude-crippling ascent of Kilimanjaro, and at others, as nerve-wracking as a sprint freeclimb of El Captain. To make it this far shows endurance, strength, skill, and fortitude.

More and more of us have now seen the view from the top and can attest it was worth the effort and what it will afford. But we can all admit, the ascent simply should not be so hard that only a few make it, and so unnecessarily arduous that some don't think it's worth trying at all. That's why no matter your elevation or how long it took you to make the climb, you can make the journey up easier for someone else. If you can look down and see someone at the foot of the mountain, let's give her the hand you wish you had, and

Send the Elevator Down!

At the beginning of 2020, the number of women in senior roles was slowly improving, says The McKinsey and LeanIn. org Women in the Workplace study. The report accounts that between January 2015 and January 2020, representation of women in senior vice president positions grew from 23 to 28 percent, and representation in the C-suite grew from 17 to 21 percent. Slim gains, but 100 percent heading in the right direction. Alas, more than a year on from the start of the pandemic these numbers are expected to plummet. Women scaling the mountain has now become the equivalent of a dangerous ascent during hail, heavy rain, and gales with no shelter in sight. The study goes to report two million women are currently considering leaving the workforce due to challenges created by COVID-19.

At the other end of the leadership spectrum though, the Women in the Workplace study also highlights that for the sixth year in a row, women have continued to lose ground at the first step up of their careers, from entry-level position to manager. That initial missed promotion ends up holding women back for their whole careers.

Rachel Thomas, CEO and cofounder of Lean In, who were also coauthor of the report, explained to me in our interview that the so-called "broken rung" is a real blind spot for the business world, which is focused more on advancing women into senior leadership roles. "Many companies are aware of the glass ceiling and are working to support women reaching the high-level senior ranks. In reality, however, women are disadvantaged from the get-go. They can't get a first foot on the ladder and then they can never catch up." In essence, the barrier women face in reaching leadership equality can be traced all the way down to that very first promotion, if and when it actually happens.

The evidence is telling. The latest LeanIn.org and McKinsey 2020 Women in the Workplace study states, for "every one hundred men promoted to manager, only eighty-five women were promoted—and this gap was even larger for some women: only fifty-eight Black women and seventy-one Latinas were promoted. As a result, women remained significantly outnumbered in entry-level management at the beginning of 2020—they held just 38 percent of manager-level positions, while men held 62 percent." And while the onus is still on organizations to fix bias in their own ranks on how young women leaders are advancing, there are some things we can do as empowered women to help them get their first step up so they can keep on climbing.

The first and most obvious step is to hire and promote her! Those statistics I pointed out should be alarming, and while there are beliefs that women are not asking for promotions and pushing themselves forward, data shared by Shelley Zalis in her 2019 article at Forbes Women says that women do, but they just don't get the same results. So, if you have the authorization, power, influence, clout, and more—advocate, sponsor, and champion that passionate and ambitious young woman on your team or in your department and help her make it to manager level. The more women who can get a foothold, the more women have a chance.

If you do not have direct abilities to make promotions and lobby others to do so, consider giving exciting new projects and assignments to the young women on your team. Shelley Zalis continues, "bias confirms women are expected to prove themselves more than their male counterparts, and are often perceived as not being ready for the next level when they are more than capable." When you award opportunities, you not only help her gain valuable experience, but you also help clearly demonstrate her abilities to others, which cannot be questioned nor denied.

Mentoring and coaching younger female members of your organization wherever possible will help her grow into a role ready for promotion. Teach her the importance of and how to grow her network and encourage her to meet with new people every week outside of your organization. In every possible way, we can be supporting her growth, her visibility, and her rise through the ranks. Taking young women just starting out under our wing, no matter at our age, can have a monumental impact not just today but far into the future.

One such woman who has made many first ascents alone, and who now spends her days lifting others, is Colonel Candice Frost. She sent the elevator down by carving a multitude of first paths for women in the US Army. Since then, she has been determined to increase the number of women in positions of leadership across the military. Candice has spoken many times of why lighting others' torches matters and shared with me, "We must all work to open doors for women, equitable representation is critical in both civilian life and the military." Candice went on, "We must be impatient for change, and we must also be the change." If we have risen to a position of power and influence, we have a responsibility, perhaps even an obligation, to pay it forward and help another woman rise. If it can be done in one of the most male-dominated professions in the world, then there is hope for us all.

In my interview with Toni Maloney, cofounder of Bpeace, she told me a story that has stayed with me ever since. It was a lesson shared with her by a former mentor, advertising tycoon David Ogilvy. He would say, "If you always hire people who are smaller than you are, we shall become a company of dwarfs. If, on the other hand, you always hire people who are bigger than you are, we shall become a company of giants." Sometimes, we have a fear of promoting and elevating someone toward a role we fought so hard to win and that's understandable. So, if you ever felt that way, try to recall Ogilvy's advice, then beyond a company of giants, maybe we can also become a world of giants with women at the center.

When I think of sending the elevator down, I have a visual image of a mountain with a chain of women stretching from the very bottom to the very top. All the way along the climb, people are helping. If there's bad weather, the climbers will find a haven. If they get lost, someone will help them back to the path. If they feel like giving up, the crowds gathering along the route will cheer them on. The more we help women rise, the more we will help women rise.

So, if opportunity isn't knocking on a sister's door, let's step it up and help her break the wall down!

CHAPTER 22

KEY #10—BE A SISTER

———

We are powerful, vibrant, strong, enduring women, and when the proverbial hits the fan—as it will at some point—we all still need a hug, a hand, and someone to listen to our troubles. This might sound trite or even patronizing to say, particularly about women, but the truth is, at one moment or another, we all need someone to care for us and give us the boost we need to help us carry on. Women I've supported needed space and time to process things happening at home that they were shouldering, such as the mental health concerns of a child or a health issue for themselves. Others wanted to unpack an unexpected performance review and better understand where they could improve. Some wanted to prep for a big project presentation or job interview they deeply wanted. For the good times and bad, everyone needs support to reach their dreams and live their best life.

As the African proverb says, "If you want to go fast, go alone. If you want to go far, go together." A sisterhood of women who come together to provide support not only helps a woman in need, but our collective actions can raise the potential for all women. When we go together, boosting each other along the way, our doubts can be extinguished, our spirits can be lifted, and our ambitions can fly.

For the days that are hard, for the days without end, and for the days that we have waited for our whole lives, hold out your hand and

Be a Sister!

It's impossible to believe we can do it all. We are already holding ourselves, our families, and our careers together. So, when the burden becomes too much to bear, a support structure is critical to ensure we can keep going and the wheels don't come flying off our wagon. But as women, we have been conditioned to be the caregivers, we are the ones selflessly rushing to support others, and rarely taking our own needs and wellness into account. We can give all day long, go to bed exhausted, and never even have a single moment for ourselves. So as you read this chapter, this one's a reminder as much for you as it is for the women you want to help. We all need to stop and practice self-care to breathe, live joy, and do the big things our lives are asking of us.

I was once at an event where I heard the feminist activist and a personal heroine of mine, Gloria Steinem, speak. She asked the audience if we were familiar with the "Golden Rule." There were lots of nods as we all contemplated in our minds the saying "Do unto others as you would have done to yourself." Gloria then asked if we knew the "Golden Rule for Women." This time, every single person shook their head and then shifted about awkwardly in their seats as she explained the "Golden Rule for Women" is to "Do unto yourself as you would do unto others!" It's the reminder we all need as women to take care of ourselves and ask for what we need.

There is a perception that independent women are not supposed to need help, and we are strong and don't have to depend on anyone. We will keep going, keep striving, and keep smiling. This is painfully true in the workplace. In 2016, research from Victoria L. Brescoll from the Department of Organizational Behavior at Yale University, reported women are already classified as emotional, and we fear showing any kind of emotion will equal weakness. For example, further research described by Quentin Fottrell in 2019 for MarketWatch, stated, "men who get angry at work are perceived as strong and decisive, while women are more likely to be regarded as hysterical—and, as such, may show more restraint than their male colleagues." Fottrell goes on to report that evidence demonstrates men and women are equally emotional at work, and it's just that women get penalized more when they do.

All this leads to a hypersensitivity at work where we dare not show our emotions and ask for help because showing the slightest crack in our armor may lead to us being perceived as less capable, less in control, and not able to manage the challenges a leadership role requires. But where does that leave us? We can't always hold everything inside. We must allow ourselves to let down our guard and express our feelings and stresses. Otherwise, we will not be able to survive in the workforce, let alone thrive.

The pandemic took an enormous toll on women. According to the LeanIn.org and McKinsey 2020 workplace study, more than five million women have lost their jobs and millions more are leaving the workforce at alarming rates pushed to the limits as they disproportionately carry the burdens of housework and child care. Some challenges are unprecedented and will require more than a shoulder to cry on. And with that being said, a shoulder at the right moment might just give a much-needed boost for them not to give up.

One of the most important things you can do for yourself and for another woman is to ask for help. By asking for help, you are indicating to a sister, regardless of what she might think, that it's okay to ask. You will show her that it's truly alright to want to share your challenges and ask for support in finding a way forward. You might want her input on how to prioritize the projects you are juggling, you might want advice on how to best delegate some tasks, you might need to vent about a colleague, or you might want to share concerns about a program going sideways. At some point, we all need someone to help us through what's going on for us. Yes, we can do it alone, but it might take longer to make happen and be more painful in the process. Furthermore, with the help of another pair of eyes and ears, your conclusions could be stronger and outcomes more impactful.

As described in the chapters on networks, women connecting, sharing, and supporting one another has shown to significantly impact their success and well-being. Lindsay Kaplan, CEO at Chief.com—the social network for women—told me, "Right now I think it's the most important thing we do as women. Not everybody in the world understands what it's like to be a high-powered executive with the stress and the toll it takes on your personal life. It's key to have people in the room who understand and create a supportive environment." That doesn't only apply to executives, regardless of your position, having someone you can connect with deeply can help you focus, understand the normal pressures of where you are at, and cocreate strategies together to advance.

When you demonstrate it's really okay not to be perfect and that even the best of us still need help, emotionally or otherwise, it sets a clear example and gives her permission to do the same. When we show up like sisters, and when we can offer everything from a kind word, a smile, a hug, some tough love, and sorority, we can help her rise to fill the space she has a right to command.

Regardless of creating workplace success, a UCLA study, shared by *Psychology Today* in 2008, has proven close female friendships improve the quality of our lives. They have been shown to help us withstand extreme stress, experience more joy-filled lives, reduce blood pressure, heart rates, and cholesterol, and even directly correlate friendships, or lack of, with mortality.

Bestselling author Sally Helgesen proposed, in November 2020 for a LinkedIn article she wrote, that women should work on leaning on each other, not "leaning in," making reference to the book and movement Sheryl Sandberg began. Sally said, "The simple truth is that we can't get through this alone. Our ability to carve a path forward requires that we engage others for support: those we love and trust, those we admire, those we find inspiring, and those who have our backs." She goes on to say that by leaning on others, we invite them to also lean on us.

We all need a network of sisters who are willing to cheer us on and celebrate our success. We need a group of women who will inspire us and encourage us forward. We need our sister's wisdom and willingness to share their feedback, advice, and ideas. We need them to hold up the mirror, as well as the torch to light our way.

And, when we finally take sisterhood into our offices and networks, the collective power of our actions and our love might just cause a revolution.

PART III

IT BEGINS AND ENDS WITH YOU

CHAPTER 23

HOW WE ALL TAKE FLIGHT

The way forward isn't a road we take,
the way forward is a road women make.

—AMANDA GORMAN

To empower another woman is a selfless act with untold possibilities. Could it be your words that make her level up her sense of worth? Could it be your actions that fundamentally changes the direction of her life? What if what you see in her, which she cannot see in herself, makes all the difference? A simple enabling step from you could well be, at its smallest point, a woman being supported, and at its peak an earth-shattering leap set in motion for us all. That's the thing when you choose to empower another woman, you never know where it might end.

One thing is certain though, to empower is also an act that solidifies our own power and presence. Where when we reach out to another woman, we too are reached. Where when we help her step forward, we too move forward. And where when we hold another woman up, we are also lifted. To empower another woman is also to empower ourselves.

In my experience, it's like getting a reverse charge, a kinetic jolt of energy that stirs our own positive momentum. Helping another woman not only makes us feel good, according to Dr. Christine L. Carter in her 2010 article for *Psychology Today*, "experiments have actually demonstrated again and again that kindness toward others actually causes us to be happier, improves our health, and lengthens our lives." Taking these generous acts can also advance our own position. As Amy J.C. Cuddy explained in 2013 for the *Harvard Business Review*, the way to influence and to lead is to begin with warmth. "Warmth is the conduit of influence: It facilitates trust and the communication and absorption of ideas. Even a few small nonverbal signals—a nod, a smile, an open gesture—can show people that you're pleased to be in their company and attentive to their concerns." It goes back to human relationships, something in the workplace that has been severely missing, and what we as women must reclaim.

The flywheel, which we mention often, is also a flywheel for our own growth and development and deepens our sense of knowledge and worth. When we get the wheel turning, everyone around us can benefit, including you. I hope in reading the ten keys you have felt encouraged to support a colleague and give her a much-needed boost. Also, I hope you felt empowered with agency and power and an ability to affect change.

You are the force that turns the keys to unlock potential, and without you, we will still be waiting. Deep-rooted change requires us all to help.

In Part I, I shared the many stories of women working to create change for all women. They focused on creating "access to voice" like Holly Gordon did for millions of girls with the global movement she founded Girls Rising, and Tracy Chou who used her single voice to encourage others and forever changed the landscape of Silicon Valley by kicking off the diversity debate in technology. Women like Toni Maloney (cofounder of the Business Council of Peace) and Fereshteh Forough (founder of Code to Inspire), who are working to give more women and girls "access to skills and opportunity," just like Colonel Candice Frost has carved a path for more women in the US Army to advance.

There were others like Lindsay Kaplan (CEO and cofounder at Chief.com), Rachel Thomas (cofounder of LeanIn.org), Kristin Libin (cofounder of HeyMama), and Kristy Wallace (CEO at Ellevate), who are helping women connect and deeply support each other forward with "access to network." And, women like Cat Berman (CEO and cofounder of CNote) and Sophie McNaught at The Shed helping women gain knowledge and "access to capital." And finally, women like Jocelyn Mangan at Him for Her, and Sharon Vosmek at Astia helping create "access to leverage" through gaining influence and maximizing opportunity.

ACCESS TO SELF

As we reach the final stretch of the book, I want to focus the last chapter specifically on you and a key element that we haven't yet discussed, "access to self." It's where it all begins and ends. Without agency and power over our own lives, how can we support others, our society, and the world? How do we empower ourselves so we can empower others?

In Maslow's hierarchy of needs theory, as stated by Neel Burton, MD for *Psychology Today* in an updated 2020 article, when the four categories of human motivations are met, it is then we can we begin to focus on self-actualization and our desire to be all that we can be. I get super excited about this moment in a person's life because through my program at The Coaching Fellowship and working with hundreds of women, I see the most change and most potential shift when women get full access to themselves. There is a reason that knowing oneself is called an awakening. We wake up to what we truly want and who we truly are, and we feel empowered to push through our self-imposed limitations.

Over the years, I have observed one more level in Maslow's theory. One where at a certain point of gaining full access to self, the hierarchy pyramid of needs inverts and reaches infinitely outward where we cannot help but support every person and every living thing to reach its full potential. When we become compelled to help, it's a beautiful cycle of rising and thriving.

Access to self begins with understanding our beliefs and values. They are what drive us every day and define what we care most about. When we spend time getting to know what is really underneath what brings us joy, fulfillment, and resonance, we will be more motivated to lead, inspired to do more, help more, and be happier in the process.

So much of access to self is about what happens on the inside. It's about listening to ourselves more acutely and gaining control of the inner critic, which can loudly override our dreams and best intentions. Our inner saboteur will keep us playing small, protect us from the harms of failure, and stop us from claiming everything we most desire. It's often easier to spot the saboteur at play in someone else than admitting to ourselves why we are really holding back.

A former teacher of mine once said, "to live your life on purpose is a radical act." I have found it to be a constant striving, or losing and forgetting, then remembering and getting back on track. To live our lives according to our values, our head and heart need to work in tandem. As when we can consciously act in favor of our most inner drivers, the weight of our decisions increases and our impact is amplified.

Just like you have read about in the ten keys for helping another woman, those same lessons are also true for us. When we can pay more attention to the wise woman who lives deep inside us who knows what's best and calls us forth, then we have access to ourselves, full power and wisdom. We too need the support of women to help us hear our inner wisdom, and the nourishing words she has to say, and believe in ourselves.

For us to thrive, we must also find the women in our lives who will help us continue and move us to the next stage. As celebrated and wise author Brené Brown said in her bestselling 2010 book, *The Gifts of Imperfection*, "Somehow we've come to equate success with not needing anyone. Many of us are willing to extend a helping hand, but we're very reluctant to reach out for help when we need it ourselves. It's as if we've divided the world into 'those who offer help' and 'those who need help.' The truth is that we are both."

Remember, by giving another woman a chance to help you, you are also giving her an opportunity to feel valued and whole. You will reinforce her worth and she will feel seen, moved into prominence, and lifted because you asked her.

The baton of empowered women passes freely between us, to whoever is in most need, and back again. It's a precious empowering cyclical gift that advances all involved and has the potential like a waterfall to cascade down to the others around us.

And that gift is all the more necessary today. Almost all indicators of women's advancement took a strong turn for the worst in 2020 because of the COVID-19 pandemic. A tiny snapshot from James Hookway in November 2020 for *The Wall Street Journal* includes: "millions of women leaving the workforce either through layoffs as they largely work in the service sector, or leaving due to necessity to care take their families, the so-called 'pink recession.'" Kamala Harris, in her 2021 opinion article for *The Washington Post*, further lamented, "one quarter of US women-owned businesses have closed," and called the mass exodus of women from the workforce a national emergency, the effects are chilling. Hookway goes on to reference one UN report that found women may have lost an entire generation of progress due to COVID-19.

So where do we go from here? How do we not only get back on track but also accelerate the progress of women and girls everywhere? That was the question I found myself asking in the summer of 2020 as the pandemic spun out of control, wildfires raged around me in the Western United States, and democracy seemed to be faltering.

What transpired was a culmination of ideas, experience, and possibilities of this book that became the container of what could be the next wave of female activism. What if women empowering women—en masse—was actually the answer? Is it the answer that would finally, and within a generation, create a surge of momentum once and for all? Can we finally take progress into our own capable and powerful hands?

REACHING A TIPPING POINT

I believe when we open up to ourselves to being a sister and to being an activist for women, something magical happens. The groundswell of energy is palpable and growing. I felt it every time I spoke with the empowered women I interviewed and with every woman I talked to about this book. There's a nerve we have hit, a way we now hear the call to help differently in our ears. It's a calling forth of what we know how to do and what we have already been doing, now to be magnified by the hundreds of thousands and millions of actions.

What happens when empowered women empowering women hits the tipping point? Exponential growth is the answer. Let's pause for just a moment and do the math. I want you to understand the implications of your actions. If you were to only help two women today and those two women would go on and each help two more women tomorrow, your impact would have already touched six women in total. If those four women do the same and each empower two more women, your impact has soared to fourteen women. But now it gets interesting, if this groundswell continues each day for fourteen days, your original empowering action would have reached more than sixteen thousand women. Four days after that, you are close to reaching every person living in the United States, and by the evening of the thirty-second day, you will have impacted every single woman on this planet. This, of course, is the deceiving math of compounding growth—and the reason why empowering others, and empowering them to empower the women in their circles, matters so much. It all seems possible and easy, doesn't it?

Can you imagine a world of millions of empowered women? Ask yourself, when millions of women ask for their worth, earn it, and choose to invest in women and minority-owned businesses—will capitalism change? If millions of women change the face of capitalism, and our economies are not solely driven by stock market and shareholder gains, but rather wealth creation for all, will that mean we have a fairer and equitable world? If millions of women share their stories and are authentically heard, seen, published, and reach a mass audience, will attitudes change and society become more inclusive with diversity welcomed? If millions more women lead countries, companies, and institutions, could the climate crisis, wars, and suffering be a thing of the past?

You understand by now that I'm a dreamer, an idealist. I love to imagine the humming sounds, and idyllic pictures of harmony and equilibrium. Maybe we won't empower every woman on Earth and solve every issue in our lifetimes, but we can transform the role and reach of women in a shorter timeframe than most of us believe. I can easily imagine a world with more empowered women where there is more balance, opportunity, and sufficiency. A world where poverty, ignorance, and hate are reduced. A world where unnecessary suffering is eliminated and resources might be equally distributed. Not a perfect world, but a more just and fair one for all.

At a TEDx Sandhill Road Women event in 2012, I heard the revered author, and activist Lynne Twist speak. I share what she said often. She spoke of a Native American prophecy that the twenty-first century will be the time when the bird of humanity realizes it has been flying with one wing. She described the state of our ailing world, missing out on its potential with women vacant from the table. With only one wing—the male wing—the bird is faltering, tired, and all around it is unstable and collapsing. In the audience, I wept as Lynne said, "when the female wing fully expresses itself, the male wing can relax, and the bird of humanity can finally soar."

What if we are indeed the ones we've been waiting for? And by doing what we inherently do best, with ease and with love, magnified and executed by the hundreds of thousands, we might start a quiet revolution in our own house, our own office, and the world. Because we are the daughters of the courageous women who came before us—all capable of greatness when we are held and encouraged. And we are each a mother in our own right, fierce advocates and caretakers of all daughters, all sons, and the earth. Empowered women empowering women is indeed more than fixing a broken wing, it is how we all take flight.

This is how we rise.

ACKNOWLEDGMENTS

Writing a book is testament to a commitment, and the conviction that one's words must live out in the world. It will also turn you inside and out, and humble you again, and again. The journey cannot be undertaken alone. During the course of writing my first book, so many people have helped empower and encourage me. They have not only made the book better; they have made what you hold in your hands possible.

First, thank you to all the powerful women interviewees who so graciously agreed to be interviewed, and who shared so openly that I might capture their authentic stories of empowering women and girls across the globe. You inspired me beyond measure, and I know your stories will inspire thousands more.

Thank you to my many early supporters who donated generously to The Coaching Fellowship and became part of my Author's Heroine Circle: Amber Smith, Amory Wakefield, Anna Ladd, Anne B. Storer, Annmarie Costelloe, Catherine Berman, Chaya Pomeranz-Sherman, Christy Kercheville,

Christy Tripp, Cindy Lima, Corinne Warnshuis, Diane Tate, Eileen Goldman, Gail Bechtold, Heather Sparks, Jacqueline Keeso, Jess Davis, Joan M. Harper, Lisa Quilici, Mary Ellen Muckerman, Melanie Doebler, Michelle Maloy Dillon, Michelle Page, Molly Pyle, Monica Phillips, Nora Delay, Patrice Beard, Samantha Rose, Skylar Gieseke, Sophia Jones, Stephanie Nguyen, Suzanne OBrien, Wendy Appel, Winnie Aoieong.

I must also deeply thank a small group of special beta readers who read early versions of the entire book, and gave critical feedback on my writing to make it better. Thank you sincerely: Athena Katsaros, Elise Rankin, Maria Saldarriaga, Magi Evans, and Sherri Rose. I could not have done it without you.

The Coaching Fellowship has been my life's work for the past seven years, and there are so many people to thank who helped bring the book to a point where it could be realized. Thank you, Cat Berman, Karen Kimsey-House, Nan Liu, Rocco Capobianco, and Skylar Gieseke. Thank you again, Athena Katsaros and Elise Rankin. To the hundreds of volunteer coaches and the now 1,100 young women social change leaders we have supported, you have showed me change is possible, and every action—no matter how small—is absolutely worth taking.

The publishing team at New Degree Press has been extraordinary in bringing my book to life in a way that honored my voice and vision. A heartfelt thank you to Chelsea Olivia, Laura (Buckley) McInley, and Brian Bies. You told me "Great books aren't written, they are rewritten!" During the "rewriting" process, your expertise, guidance, and kindness brought a humble manuscript to full life.

The highest praise goes to Eric Koester and his team at Georgetown's Creator Institute. Thank you, Eric, for democratizing access to publishing, and supporting first-time authors like me. Without your genesis, thousands of stories would be left untold.

Finally, thank you dear Pascal Finette. You lived with "Hemingway mode" for nine months! You gave me time and space, helped me read, and research, you are my true partner in every sense of the world. You have empowered me as a woman from the moment we met. A final thank you to my strong, smart, and beautiful mum, Kathy Hatton. COVID-19 has kept an ocean between us for too long, but your empowering ways, my whole life long, means we are still completely as one. There's a part of you in everything I do.

Jane Finette

APPENDIX

INTRODUCTION

British Library. "Timeline of the Women's Liberation Movement." 2021. https://www.bl.uk/sisterhood/timeline.

Britannica, T. Editors of Encyclopedia. "Women's suffrage." *Encyclopedia Britannica*, September 10, 2020. https://www.britannica.com/topic/woman-suffrage.

Miller, Bruce dir. The Handmaid's Tale (TV series). Aired April 26, 2017, on Hulu. https://www.imdb.com/title/tt5834204.

O'Reilly, Marie. "Why Women? Inclusive Security and Peaceful Societies." *Inclusive Security*, October 2015. https://www.inclusivesecurity.org/publication/why-women-inclusive-security-and-peaceful-societies.

Pfeffer, Leticia. "10 Reasons Why Investing in Women and Girls Is So Important." *Global Citizen*, July 9, 2014. https://www.globalcitizen.org/en/content/10-reasons-why-investing-in-women-and-girls-is-so.

The Coaching Fellowship. "Fellows Page." Accessed June 12, 2021. https://tcfs.org/fellows.

The Rainforest Alliance. "Women Are the Key to Environmental Resilience." March 8, 2020. https://www.rainforest-alliance. org/articles/women-are-the-key-to-environmental-resilience.

Thomas, Gerald, director. *Carry On*. Aired August 1, 1958, on BBC. https://www.comedy.co.uk/guide/group/carry_on.

Topping, Alexandra. "Endemic Violence against Women Is Causing a Wave of Anger." *The Guardian*, March 11, 2021. https://www.theguardian.com/world/2021/mar/11/endemic-violence-against-women-is-causing-a-wave-of-anger.

USAID. "Fact Sheet - Food Security and Gender." Accessed June 12, 2021. https://www.oecd.org/dac/gender-development/46460857. pdf.

USAID. "10 Reasons Why Investing in Women and Girls Is So Important." May 5, 2020. https://www.usaid.gov/what-we-do/ gender-equality-and-womens-empowerment/womens-economic-empowerment.

World Economic Forum. "Global Gender Gap Report 2020." 2021. http://www3.weforum.org/docs/WEF_GGGR_2020.pdf.

CHAPTER 1

BBC. "'Harmful' Gender Stereotypes in Adverts Banned." *New York Times*, 14 June 2019. https://www.bbc.com/news/business-48628678.

Broomfield, Matt. "Women's March against Donald Trump Is the Largest Day of Protests in US History, Say Political Scientists." *The Independent,* January 23, 2017. https://www.independent.co.uk/news/world/americas/womens-march-anti-donald-trump-womens-rights-largest-protest-demonstration-us-history-political-scientists-a7541081.html.

Das, Andrew. "US Women's Soccer Team Sues US Soccer for Gender Discrimination." *New York Times*, March 8, 2019. https://www.nytimes.com/2019/03/08/sports/womens-soccer-team-lawsuit-gender-discrimination.html.

Doherty, Maggie. "The Forgotten Feminists of the Backlash Decade." *New Republic*, September 24, 2020. https://newrepublic.com/article/159234/history-forgotten-feminists-1990s-levenstein-book-review.

Doward, Jamie and Tali Fraser. "Hollywood's Gender Pay Gap Revealed: Male Stars Earn $1m More Per Film Than Women." *The Guardian*, September 15, 2019. https://www.theguardian.com/world/2019/sep/15/hollywoods-gender-pay-gap-revealed-male-stars-earn-1m-more-per-film-than-women.

Dunbar, Brian. "Friday's All-Woman Spacewalk: The Basics." *NASA*, October 17, 2019. https://www.nasa.gov/feature/fridays-all-woman-spacewalk-the-basics.

Human Rights Campaign. "Marriage Equality Around the World." Accessed June 12, 2021. https://www.hrc.org/resources/marriage-equality-around-the-world.

Levenstein, Lisa. *They Didn't See Us Coming: The Hidden History of Feminism in the Nineties.* New York: Basic Books, 2020.

Me Too. "About page." Accessed June 12, 2021. https://metoomvmt.org.

Nugent, Annabel. "Halle Berry Calls Her Historic Oscar Win 'One of My Biggest Heartbreaks'." *The Independent*, September 10, 2020. https://www.independent.co.uk/arts-entertainment/films/news/halle-berry-oscar-win-heartbreak-monsters-ball-b421387.html.

Planned Parenthood. "Birth Control Has Expanded Opportunity for Women — In Economic Advancement, Educational Attainment, and Health Outcomes." June 2015. https://www.plannedparenthood.org/files/1614/3275/8659/BC_factsheet_may2015_updated_1.pdf.

Salam, Maya. "Americans' Shifting Attitude on Gay Rights." *New York Times*, June 18, 2019. https://www.nytimes.com/2019/06/18/us/americans-lgbt-opinions.html.

Shipman, Claire, Katty Kay, and JillEllyn Riley. "How Puberty Kills Girls' Confidence." *The Atlantic*, September 20, 2018. https://www.theatlantic.com/family/archive/2018/09/puberty-girls-confidence/563804.

Smiltneek, Elizabeth. "Suffrage Movement." *Learning to Live.* Accessed June 12, 2021. https://www.learningtogive.org/resources/suffrage-movement.

The History Channel. "Women's March." January 2017. https://www.history.com/this-day-in-history/womens-march.

The New York Times. "Full Coverage: Harvey Weinstein Is Found Guilty of Rape." February 24, 2020. https://www.nytimes.com/2020/02/24/nyregion/harvey-weinstein-verdict.html.

The Whitehouse. "Kamala Harris." Accessed June 12, 2021. https://www.whitehouse.gov/administration/vice-president-harris.

UN Women. "Emma Watson: Gender Equality Is Your Issue Too." September 20, 2014. https://www.unwomen.org/en/news/stories/2014/9/emma-watson-gender-equality-is-your-issue-too.

Viebeck, Elise. "Joe Biden Was in Charge of the Anita Hill Hearing. Even He Says It Wasn't Fair." *The Washington Post,* April 26, 2019. https://www.washingtonpost.com/politics/joe-biden-was-in-charge-of-the-anita-hill-hearing-even-he-says-it-wasnt-fair/2019/04/26/a9a6f384-6500-11e9-82ba-fcfeff232e8f_story.html.

Wakefield, Jane. "The Tech Billionaire Who Is Putting Women First." *BBC,* April 7, 2021. https://www.bbc.com/news/technology-56662100.

Weaver, Caity. "The Spice Girls Generation: Uniting All Women in the Pursuit of Girl Power." *The Independent,* August 4, 2019. https://www.independent.co.uk/arts-entertainment/spice-girls-tour-girl-power-comeback-feminism-geri-halliwell-emma-bunton-a9018946.html.

Women's March. "Mission Page." Accessed June 12, 2021. https://womensmarch.com/mission-and-principles.

CHAPTER 2

Adler, Lou. "New Survey Reveals 85% of All Jobs Are Filled Via Networking" *LinkedIn*, February 28, 2016. https://www.linkedin.com/pulse/new-survey-reveals-85-all-jobs-filled-via-networking-lou-adler/?trk=prof-post.

Casciaro, Tiziana, Francesca Gino, and Maryam Kouchaki. "The Contaminating Effects of Building Instrumental Ties: How Networking Can Make Us Feel Dirty." *Sage Journals*, October 6, 2014.https://journals.sagepub.com/doi/full/10.1177/0001839214554990.

Chief. "Homepage." Accessed May 27, 2021. https://www.chief.com.

Chuluun, Tuugi and Kevin L. Young. "Women at the Top of the World, Still Not at the Center." *The Brookings Institution*, December 2020. https://www.brookings.edu/essay/women-at-the-top-of-the-world-still-not-at-the-center-a-new-network-analysis-discovery.

Crook, Jordan. "Chief, the Leadership Network for Women, Raises $15 Million in Funding." *TechCrunch,* May 21, 2020. https://techcrunch.com/2020/05/21/chief-the-leadership-network-for-women-raises-15-million-in-funding.

Ellevate Network. "About Page." Accessed May 27, 2021. https://www.ellevatenetwork.com/about.

Ibarra, Herminia. "Why Strategic Networks Are Important for Women and How to Build Them." *EVE Program*, September 27, 2017. https://www.eveprogramme.com/en/30217/strategic-networks.

Mancuso Tradenta, Julio, Ananta Neelim, and Joe Vecci. "Gender Differences in Self-Promotion: Understanding the Female Modesty Constraint." *SSRN*, December 29, 2017. https://papers.ssrn.com/sol3/papers.cfm?abstract_id=3039233.

Newcomb, Alyssa. "Record Number of Women Took over Fortune 500 Companies in 2020." *NBC News*, December 30, 2020. https://www.nbcnews.com/business/business-news/record-number-women-took-over-fortune-500-companies-2020-n1252491.

Pfeffer, Jeffrey. "Networking Is a Critical Skill—Learn to Do It Even During a Pandemic." *Cornerstone,* October 29, 2020. https://www.cornerstoneondemand.com/rework/networking-critical-skill%E2%80%94learn-do-it-even-during-pandemic.

Sherberg, Ellen. "In Her Own Words: Lindsay Kaplan, Co-founder of Chief, a Private Network for Powerful Women, Sees Herself as a Stay-at-Home Mom. It's Hard Work." *BizJournals,* May 20, 2020. https://www.bizjournals.com/bizwomen/news/latest-news/2020/04/in-her-own-words-lindsay-kaplan-co-founder-of.html?page=all.

X. "Homepage." Accessed May 27, 2021. https://x.company.

CHAPTER 3

Ayubi, Najla. "Women's Biggest Problems in Afghanistan." *The Asia Foundation*, January 27, 2010. https://asiafoundation.org/2010/01/27/womens-biggest-problems-in-afghanistan-2.

BPeace. "About Page." Accessed May 30, 2021. https://www.bpeace. org//#whatwedo.

Hudson, Valerie M., Donna Lee Bowen, and Perpetua Lynne Nielsen. "We Are Not Helpless. Addressing Structural Gender Inequality in Post-Conflict Societies." *Inclusive Security,* 2016. https://www.inclusivesecurity.org/wp-content/ uploads/2016/03/We-are-not-helpless.pdf.

Human Rights Watch. "Girls' Access to Education in Afghanistan." 2017. https://www.hrw.org/report/2017/10/17/i-wont-be-doctor-and-one-day-youll-be-sick/girls-access-education-afghanistan.

Niethammer, Carmen. "Women, Peace and Security - Challenges and Opportunities in Light of the Corona Pandemic." *Forbes,* April 4, 2020. https://www.forbes.com/sites/ carmenniethammer/2020/04/04/women-peace-and-securitychallenges-and-opportunities-in-light-of-the-corona-pandemic/?sh=267cab2162eb.

Rehn, Elisabeth and Ellen Johnson Sirleaf. "Women, War and Peace: The Independent Experts' Assessment on the Impact of Armed Conflict on Women and Women's Role in Peace-Building." *Consortium on Gender, Security, & Human Rights,* 2002. https://genderandsecurity.org/sites/default/files/Rehn_Sirleaf_-_W_War_Peace_-_the_Independent_Experts_Assessment_on_the_Impact_of_AC_on_W_Ws_Role_in_Pbldg.pdf.

Salary Explorer. "Average Salary in Afghanistan 2021." Accessed May 30, 2021. http://www.salaryexplorer.com/salary-survey. php?loc=1&loctype=1.

Takahashi, Dean. "Code to Inspire Trains Girls to Code and Make Games in Afghanistan." *VentureBeat*, April 15, 2019. https://venturebeat.com/2019/04/15/fereshteh-forough-interview.

The World Bank. "Female Entrepreneurship Resource Point - Introduction and Module 1: Why Gender Matters." 2021. https://www.worldbank.org/en/topic/gender/publication/female-entrepreneurship-resource-point-introduction-and-module-1-why-gender-matters.

United Nations, Office of the Special Adviser on Gender Issues and Advancement of Women. "Landmark Resolution on Women, Peace and Security." 2021. https://www.un.org/womenwatch/osagi/wps.

United Nations. "United Nationals Sustainable Development Goals, Goal 5: Gender Equity." https://www.un.org/sustainabledevelopment/gender-equality.

USAID. "Women's Global Development and Prosperity (w-gdp) Fund Announces $122 Million in Progress and Partnerships." September 3, 2020. https://www.usaid.gov/w-gdp/fact-sheet/aug-2020-womens-global-development-and-prosperity-fund-announces-122m-progress-partnerships.

CHAPTER 4

BBC. "Uber Investigated over Gender Discrimination." 2018. https://www.bbc.com/news/business-44852852.

Chou, Tracy. "Where Are the Numbers?" *Medium*, October 11, 2013. https://medium.com/@triketora/where-are-the-numbers-cb997a57252.

Chou, Tracy. "Why Female Founders Will Outlast the Men." *Marker*, February 21, 2020. https://marker.medium.com/why-female-founders-will-outlast-the-men-fc379dcd6f0c.

Delventhal, Shoshanna. "How Quora Works and Makes Money." *The Atlantic*, May 15, 2020. https://www.investopedia.com/articles/investing/041916/how-quora-works-and-makes-money.asp.

Dickey, Megan Rose. "VC Firms Need to Release Portfolio Diversity Data." *TechCrunch*, February 15, 2020. https://techcrunch.com/2020/02/15/vc-firms-need-to-release-portfolio-diversity-data.

Eadicicco, Lisa. "Silicon Valley Has a Huge Diversity Problem and These Charts Prove It." *Business Insider,* July 9, 2014. https://www.businessinsider.com/diversity-in-tech-2014-2014-7.

Finette, Jane. "Learn More about the Success of Our Amazing Coaching Fellows." *The Coaching Fellowship*, May 24, 2016. https://read.thecoachingfellowship.org/learn-more-about-the-success-of-our-amazing-coaching-fellows-bc798f1ea73f.

Grace Hopper Celebration. "Homepage." Accessed May 30, 2021. https://ghc.anitab.org.

Gutman, Rachel. "The Origins of Diversity Data in Tech." *The Atlantic*, February 3,2018. https://www.theatlantic.com/

technology/archive/2018/02/the-origins-of-diversity-da-ta-in-tech/552155.

Hayes, Adam. "FAAMG Stocks." *Investopedia*, November 23, 2020. https://www.investopedia.com/terms/f/faamg-stocks.asp.

Heller, Nathan. "How Pinterest Engineer Tracy Chou Is Break-ing the Silicon Ceiling." *Vogue Magazine*, November 21, 2014. https://www.vogue.com/article/pinterest-tracy-chou-sili-con-valley.

Hempel, Jessi. "Quantifying Silicon Valley's Diversity Issue." *Wired Magazine*, April 21, 2015. https://www.wired.com/2015/04/tra-cy-chou.

Isaac, Mike. "Women in Tech Band Together to Track Diversity, After Hours." *New York Times*, May 3, 2016. https://www.nytimes.com/2016/05/04/technology/women-in-tech-band-together-to-track-diversity-after-hours.html?_r=0.

Katz, Mirander. "This Twenty-Something Forced Silicon Valley to 'Show Her the Numbers.'" *The Atlantic*, October 14, 2015. https://www.wired.com/2016/10/this-twenty-something-forced-silicon-valley-to-show-her-the-numbers.

Lazzaro, Sage. "12 Statistics about Women in Tech That Show How Big the Gender Gap Truly Is." *The Observer*, May 6, 2017. https://observer.com/2017/06/women-in-tech-statistics.

Mundy, Liz. "Why Is Silicon Valley So Awful to Women?" *The Atlantic*, April 2017. https://www.theatlantic.com/magazine/archive/2017/04/why-is-silicon-valley-so-awful-to-women/517788.

Pao, Ellen. "Homepage." Accessed May 30, 2021. https://www.ellenkpao.com.

Pistilli, Melissa. "10 Top Technology Stocks by Market Cap." *Investing News Network,* November 19, 2020. https://investingnews.com/daily/tech-investing/top-technology-stocks.

Price, Helena. "Tracy Chou." *Techies,* January 31, 2016. https://techiesproject.com/tracy-chou.

Project Include. "Homepage." Accessed May 30, 2021. https://projectinclude.org.

Rodriguez, Salvador. "Why Silicon Valley Is Failing Miserably at Diversity, and What Should Be Done About It." *International Business Times,* June 7, 2015. https://www.ibtimes.com/why-silicon-valley-failing-miserably-diversity-what-should-be-done-about-it-1998144.

Rooney, Kate and Yasmin Khorram. "Tech Companies Say They Value Diversity, but Reports Show Little Change in Last Six Years." *CNBC,* June 12, 2020. https://www.cnbc.com/2020/06/12/six-years-into-diversity-reports-big-tech-has-made-little-progress.html.

Sabin, Sam. "'No One's Accountable': Why Silicon Valley Struggles to Diversify Its Workforce." *Morning Consult,* June 11, 2020.

https://morningconsult.com/2020/06/11/silicon-valley-tech-diversity.

Winegarner, Beth. "How Ellen Pao Lost Her Job but Survived Reddit's Swamp of Trolls." *The Guardian*, July 12, 2015. https://www.theguardian.com/technology/2015/jul/12/ellen-pao-reddit-trolls-feminist-silicon-valley.

CHAPTER 5

ABC News. "Peter Jennings." Accessed May 30, 2021. https://abcnews.go.com/WNT/story?id=126542.

Begley Bloom, Laura. "How One Woman Is Starting a Menstrual Revolution in Kenya." *Forbes*, August 31, 2018. https://www.forbes.com/sites/laurabegleybloom/2018/08/31/woman-starting-menstrual-revolution-kenya/?sh=453027a62044.

Campbell, Olivia. "Tools for Change." *Harvard Magazine*, July/August 2016. https://www.harvardmagazine.com/2016/07/tools-for-change.

Cole, Diane. "6 Young Women Went to the U.N. With a Bill of Rights for Girls." *NPR*, October 11, 2019. https://www.npr.org/sections/goatsandsoda/2019/10/11/769264644/6-young-women-went-to-the-u-n-with-a-bill-of-rights-for-global-girls.

Epstein, Daniel. "World's First Accelerator Dedicated to Impacting Millions of Girls in Poverty." *Unreasonable Group*, January 14, 2015. https://unreasonablegroup.com/articles/worlds-first-accelerator-dedicated-to-impacting-millions-of-girls-in-poverty.

Girl Rising. "Girl Rising Impact Highlights." Accessed May 30, 2021. https://static1.squarespace.com/static/54aeb989e4b02736a774d-d68/t/5a9f552571c10bf6d3720e09/1520391462745/IWD_Impact-1Pager.pdf.

Girl Rising the Film. "Homepage." Accessed May 30, 2021. https://girlrising.org/the-film.

Girls Bill of Rights. "Homepage." Accessed May 30, 2021. https://www.girlsbillofrights.org.

Her Journey to School. "Homepage." Accessed May 30, 2021. https://herjourneytoschool.org.

Kwauk, Christina and Amanda Braga. "Three Platforms for Girls' Education in Climate Strategies." *The Brookings Institution*, October 11, 2019. https://www.brookings.edu/wp-content/uploads/2017/09/platforms-for-girls-education-in-climate-strategies.pdf.

MAIA Impact. "Homepage." Accessed May 30, 2021. https://www.maiaimpact.org.

Malala Fund. "Malala Fund Releases Report on Girls' Education and COVID-19." April 6, 2020. https://malala.org/newsroom/archive/malala-fund-releases-report-girls-education-covid-19.

Malala Fund. "Malala's Story." Accessed May 30, 2021. https://malala.org/malalas-story.

McClure, Alecia. "Eliakunda: The Best Version of Herself." *Africa Aid*, July 17, 2017. https://africaid.org/eliakunda-the-best-version-of-herself.

Sax, David. "The Girl Effect Accelerator Launches, Aiming to Help Girls Earning Less Than $2 a Day." *Fast Company*, October 7, 2014. https://www.fastcompany.com/3036691/for-girls-living-on-2-a-day-the-nike-foundation-launches-the-girl-effec.

She's the First. "Impact Page." Accessed May 30, 2021. https://shesthefirst.org/impact.

The Coaching Fellowship. "Fellows Page." Accessed May 30, 2021. https://www.tcfs.org/fellows.

The Girl Effect Accelerator. "Homepage." Accessed May 30, 2021. https://unreasonablegroup.com/initiatives/girl-effect-accelerator.

The Global Women's Institute. "School-Based Interventions to Prevent Violence Against Women & Girls." 2016. https://globalwomensinstitute.gwu.edu/sites/g/files/zaxdzs1356/f/downloads/Evidence%20Brief-%20School-Based%20Interventions%20to%20Prevent%20Violence%20Against%20Women%20and%20Girls.pdf.

UNICEF. Girls' Education Program. "Homepage." Accessed May 30, 2021. https://www.unicef.org/education/girls-education.

UNICEF. "10 Million Additional Girls at Risk of Child Marriage Due to COVID-19." March 8, 2021. https://www.unicef.org/

press-releases/10-million-additional-girls-risk-child-marriage-due-covid-19.

United Nations Girls Education Initiative. "Poverty Is Sexist: Why Educating Every Girl Is Good for Everyone." Accessed May 30, 2021. https://www.ungei.org/publication/poverty-sexist-why-educating-every-girl-good-everyone.

United Nations Office of the Secretary-General's Envoy on Youth. "Homepage." Accessed May 30, 2021. https://www.un.org/youthenvoy/2013/09/child-marriages-39000-every-day-more-than-140-million-girls-will-marry-between-2011-and-2020.

USAID Girls' Education. "Homepage." Accessed May 30, 2021. https://www.usaid.gov/education/girls.

ZanaAfrica. "Founders Story." Accessed May 30, 2021. http://www.zanaafrica.org/founders-story.

ZanaAfrica. "Homepage." Accessed May 30, 2021. http://www.zanaafrica.org.

ZanaAfrica. "Reach to Date." Accessed May 30, 2021. http://www.zanaafrica.org/reach-to-date.

CHAPTER 6

Borovitz, Abby. "Now, Women Can Serve in Combat." *MSNBC*, January 23, 2013. https://www.msnbc.com/the-cycle/now-women-can-serve-combat-msna18121.

Business Council of Peace Women Forward. "Homepage." Accessed May 31, 2021. https://www.bpeace.org/women-forward.

Colonel Candid. "Homepage." Accessed May 31, 2021. https://colonelcandid.com/about.

Council of Foreign Relations. "Demographics of the US Military." July 13, 2020. https://www.cfr.org/backgrounder/demographics-us-military.

Cox, Matthew. "Army Will Soon Open More Combat Jobs to Women, General Says." *Military.com*, May 24, 2019. https://www.military.com/daily-news/2019/05/24/army-will-soon-open-more-combat-jobs-women-general-says.html.

Haring, Ellen. "Meet the Quiet Trailblazers." *Army Times*, May 3, 2021. https://www.armytimes.com/opinion/commentary/2020/05/03/meet-the-quiet-trailblazer.

Maloney, Toni, and Joan Harper. *Women Forward: The 2020 Playbook*. Southampton: Business Council for Peace, 2020.

Newman, Lily Hay. "The Opportunities—and Obstacles—for Women at NSA and Cyber Command." *Wired Magazine*, April 6, 2021. https://www.wired.com/story/women-cybersecurity-nsa-cyber-command.

Powers, Rod. "Children of Military Couples and Military Single Parents." *The Balance Everyday*, November 7, 2019. https://www.thebalanceeveryday.com/what-about-the-children-3332640.

Rempfer, Kyle. "The Army Needs Thousands More Infantrymen by Spring." *Army Times*, July 29, 2019. https://www.armytimes.com/news/your-army/2019/07/29/the-army-needs-thousands-more-infantrymen-by-spring.

Smith, Stewart. "US Military Enlistment Standards for Single Parents." *The Balance Careers*, November 7, 2019. https://www.thebalancecareers.com/us-military-enlistment-standards-single-parents-3354014.

The Cycle Staff. "Today on The Cycle: Undaunted. On January 23, 2013, Pentagon Chief Leon Panetta Lifted a Ban That Prohibited Women from Serving in Combat Opening up Thousands of Front Line Positions." *MSNBC*, February 5, 2013. https://www.msnbc.com/the-cycle/today-the-cycle-undaunted-msna18546.

82nd Airborne Division. "Homepage." Accessed May 31, 2021. https://www.army.mil/82ndairborne.

CHAPTER 7

Campoamor, Danielle. "The Power of Community Is Giving HeyMama CEO Katya Libin Hope." *HeyMama*, 2021. https://heymama.co/the-power-of-community-is-giving-hey-mama-ceo-katya-libin-hope.

Congress.Gov. "H.R.866 - Fairness for Breastfeeding Mothers Act of 2019." Accessed June 1, 2021. https://www.congress.gov/bill/116th-congress/house-bill/866.

Crook, Jourdan. "HeyMama, a Premium Social Network for Moms, Raises $2 Million." *TechCrunch*, January 29, 2020. https://techcrunch.com/2020/01/29/heymama-a-premium-social-network-for-working-moms-raises-2-million.

Dickler, Jessica. "First-Time Moms See a 30% Drop in Pay. For Dads, There's a Bump Up." *CNBC*, April 30, 2019. https://www.cnbc.com/2019/04/30/first-time-moms-see-a-30percent-drop-in-pay-for-dads-theres-a-bump-up.html.

Dundas, Camille. "Why Black Women Are Still Cringing at the Lean in Strategy." *People of Color in Tech*, 2018. https://peopleofcolorintech.com/articles/why-black-women-are-still-cringing-at-the-lean-in-strategy.

Evans Ogden, Lesley. "Working Mothers Face a 'Wall' of Bias—but There Are Ways to Push Back." *Science Magazine*, April 10, 2019. https://www.sciencemag.org/careers/2019/04/working-mothers-face-wall-bias-there-are-ways-push-back.

Fried, Ina. "Tech Firms Pledge to Support Working Parents During Coronavirus Crisis." *Axios*, March 18, 2020. https://www.axios.com/tech-companies-working-parents-coronavirus-cleo-576198cc-2127-4962-9713-2d2f21ec611f.html.

Gibson, Caitlin. "The End of Leaning in: How Sheryl Sandberg's Message of Empowerment Fully Unraveled." *Forbes*, December 20, 2018. https://www.washingtonpost.com/lifestyle/style/the-end-of-lean-in-how-sheryl-sandbergs-message-of-empowerment-fully-unraveled/2018/12/19/9561eb06-fe2e-11e8-862a-b6a6f3ce8199_story.html.

Glynn, Sarah Jane. "Breadwinning Mothers Continue to Be the US Norm." *Center for American Progress*, May 10, 2019. https://www.americanprogress.org/issues/women/reports/2019/05/10/469739/breadwinning-mothers-continue-u-s-norm.

Gurley Brown, Helen. *Having It All: Love, Success, Sex, Money Even If You're Starting with Nothing.* New York: Simon & Schuster, 1982.

Guynn, Jessica. "Sheryl Sandberg: Four Years after 'Lean in' Women Are Not Better Off." *USA Today*, March 29, 2017. https://hbr.org/2019/06/research-women-score-higher-than-men-in-most-leadership-skills.

Hess, Cynthia, Tanima Ahmed, and Jeff Hayes. "Providing Unpaid Household and Care Work in the United States: Uncovering Inequality." *Institute for Women's Policy Research,* January 2020. https://iwpr.org/wp-content/uploads/2020/01/IWPR-Providing-Unpaid-Household-and-Care-Work-in-the-United-States-Uncovering-Inequality.pdf.

Hey Mama. "Announcing HeyMama x Lincoln 2021 Partnership." Accessed June 1, 2021. https://heymama.co/announcing-heymama-x-lincoln-2020-partnership.

Hey Mama. "Homepage." Accessed June 1, 2021. https://heymama.co/about-heymama.

Joseph, Shelcy V. "What New Mothers Should Know Before Re-Entering the Workforce." *Forbes*, March 16, 2020. https://www.forbes.com/sites/shelcyvjoseph/2020/03/16/what-new-mothers-should-know-before-re-entering-the-work-force/?sh=5feecb1e5891.

Kerby, Sophia. "Pay Equity and Single Mothers of Color." *Center for American Progress*, April 16, 2012. https://www.american-progress.org/issues/race/news/2012/04/16/11436/pay-equity-and-single-mothers-of-color.

Lean In. "About Page" Accessed June 1, 2021. https://leanin.org/about.

New America. "Anne-Marie Slaughter." Accessed June 1, 2021. https://www.newamerica.org/our-people/anne-marie-slaughter.

Newcomb, Alyssa. "Record Number of Women Took over Fortune 500 Companies in 2020." *NBC News*, December 30, 2020. https://www.nbcnews.com/business/business-news/record-number-women-took-over-fortune-500-companies-2020-n1252491.

Robinson, Bryan. "Pregnancy Discrimination in the Workplace Affects Mother and Baby Health." *Forbes*, July 11, 2020. https://www.forbes.com/sites/bryanrobinson/2020/07/11/pregnancy-discrimination-in-the-workplace-affects-mother-and-baby-health/?sh=496a20eacac6.

Sandberg, Sheryl. *Lean In: Women, Work, and the Will to Lead.* New York: Knopf, 2012.

Shappet, Marie-Claire. "Seriously, Why Are We Still Asking If Women Can 'Have It All'?" *Glamour Magazine*, March 20, 2019.

https://www.glamourmagazine.co.uk/article/can-women-have-it-all.

Slaughter, Anne-Marie. "Why Women Still Can't Have It All." *The Atlantic*, July/August 2012. https://www.theatlantic.com/maga-zine/archive/2012/07/why-women-still-cant-have-it-all/309020.

United Nations Population Fund. "COVID-19: A Gender Lens. Protecting Sexual and Reproductive Health and Rights, and Promoting Gender Equality." March 2020. https://www.unfpa.org/sites/default/files/resource-pdf/ COVID-19_A_Gender_Lens_Guidance_Note.pdf.

US Bureau of Labor Statistics. "Economic News Release." Accessed June 1, 2021. https://www.bls.gov/news.release/empsit.t02.htm.

US Bureau of Labor Statistics. "The Employment Situation April 2021." May 7, 2021. https://www.bls.gov/news.release/pdf/emp-sit.pdf.

Wallmine. "Sheryl Sandberg Net Worth." Accessed June 1, 2021. https://wallmine.com/people/9260/sheryl-sandberg.

Zenger, Jack and Joseph Folkman. "Research: Women Score Higher Than Men in Most Leadership Skills." *Harvard Business Review*, June 25, 2019. https://hbr.org/2019/06/research-women-score-higher-than-men-in-most-leadership-skills.

CHAPTER 8
Ada Initiative. "Homepage." Accessed June 6, 2021. https://adaini-tiative.org.

Andreessen, Marc. "Mitchell Baker." *TIME Magazine*, April 18, 2005. http://content.time.com/time/specials/packages/article/0,28804,1972656_1972712_1974235,00.html.

Baker, Mitchell. "International Women's Day; Time to Take Action." *Lizard Wrangling - Mitchell on Mozilla & More* (blog), March 7, 2016. https://blog.lizardwrangler.com/2016/03/07/international-womens-day-time-to-take-action.

Baker, Mitchell. "Living with Diverse Perspectives." *Lizard Wrangling - Mitchell on Mozilla & More* (blog), September 23, 2016. https://blog.lizardwrangler.com/2016/09/23/living-with-diverse-perspectives.

Baker, Mitchell. "Mozilla Marks 20th Anniversary with Commitment to Better Human Experiences Online." *Mozilla* (blog), March 29, 2018. https://blog.mozilla.org/en/mozilla/mozilla-marks-20th-anniversary-commitment-better-human-experiences-online.

Beard, Chris. "Diversity and Inclusion at Mozilla." *Mozilla* (blog), April 19, 2018. https://blog.mozilla.org/careers/diversity-and-inclusion-at-mozilla.

Castrillon, Caroline. "Why Women-Led Companies Are Better for Employees." *Forbes*, March 24, 2019. https://www.forbes.com/sites/carolinecastrillon/2019/03/24/why-women-led-companies-are-better-for-employees/?sh=54a6ca1b3264.

Google X Project Wing. "Homepage." Accessed June 6, 2021. https://x.company/projects/wing.

Grace Hopper Conference. "Homepage." Accessed June 6, 2021. https://ghc.anitab.org.

Internet Hall of Fame. "2012 Inductees." Accessed June 6, 2021. https://www.internethalloffame.org//inductees/year/2012.

Kramer, Anna. "They Left Mozilla to Make the Internet Better. Now They're Spreading Its Gospel for a New Generation." *Protocol*, January 29, 2021. https://www.protocol.com/mozilla-employees.

Kuchler, Hannah. "Google's Obi Felten: 'You Can't Cast Half the Population as Villains and the Other Half as the Victims'." *Financial Times*, December 5, 2018. https://www.ft.com/content/1e336774-f827-11e8-af46-2022a0b02a6c.

LeanIn.org. "Women in the Workplace 2015 Report." September 30, 2015. https://leanin.org/news-inspiration/women-in-the-workplace-2015.

LeanIn.org. "Women in the Workplace 2020 Report." Accessed June 6, 2021. https://wiw-report.s3.amazonaws.com/Women_in_the_Workplace_2020.pdf.

Montag, Ali. "'Shark Tank' Star Kevin O'Leary: Women-Run Businesses Make Me the Most Money—Here's Why." *CNBC*, March 22, 2018. https://www.cnbc.com/2018/03/22/shark-tanks-kevin-oleary-women-make-me-the-most-money.html.

Newcomb, Alyssa. "Record Number of Women Took over Fortune 500 Companies in 2020." *NBC News*, December 30, 2020. https://www.nbcnews.com/business/business-news/

record-number-women-took-over-fortune-500-companies-2020-n1252491.

Outreachy. "Homepage." Accessed June 6, 2021. https://www.outreachy.org.

TechWomen. "Homepage." Accessed June 6, 2021. https://www.techwomen.org/program/overview.

UN Secretary-General's High-Level Panel on Women's Economic Empowerment. "Panel Members." Accessed June 6, 2021. https://hlp-wee.unwomen.org/en/about/panel-members.

CHAPTER 9

Baghai, Pooneh, Olivia Howard, Lakshmi Prakash, and Jill Zucker. "Women as the Next Wave of Growth in US Wealth Management." *McKinsey*, July 29, 2020. https://www.mckinsey.com/industries/financial-services/our-insights/women-as-the-next-wave-of-growth-in-us-wealth-management.

Blow, Marla. "Statement for the Record of Marla Blow before the House Financial Services Subcommittee on Financial Services and Consumer Credit." *Consumer Financial Protection Bureau*, June 29, 2012. https://www.consumerfinance.gov/about-us/newsroom/prepared-remarks-of-marla-blow-before-the-house-financial-services-subcommittee-on-financial-services-and-consumer-credit.

Cision. "SXSW Super Accelerator Names CNote 2017 Best Startup Pitch Company." March 14, 2017. https://www.prnewswire.

com/news-releases/sxsw-super-accelerator-names-cnote-2017-best-startup-pitch-company-300423367.html.

CNote. "Cinde Dolphin – Kili Medical Drain Carrier – From Cancer Survivor to Inventor." March 8, 2018. https://www.mycnote.com/blog/cinde-dolphin-kili-medical-drain-carrier-from-patient-to-inventor.

CNote. "Homepage." Accessed June 7, 2021. https://www.mycnote.com.

Hicks, Coryanne. "Ellevest Co-Founder Sallie Krawcheck Helps Women Invest." *US News*, January 7, 2019. https://money.usnews.com/investing/investing-101/articles/ellevest-co-founder-helps-women-invest.

KILI. "Homepage." Accessed June 7, 2021. https://medicaldraincarrier.com.

Mastercard Center for Inclusive Growth. "Homepage." Accessed June 7, 2021. https://www.mastercardcenter.org.

Medici, Andy. "She Raised $40M for Her Last Startup. Here's Her New Gig." *Washington Business Journal*, October 21, 2019. https://www.bizjournals.com/washington/news/2019/10/21/she-raised-40m-for-her-last-startup-heres-where.html.

PayScale. "The State of the Gender Pay Gap in 2021 Report." 2021. https://www.payscale.com/data/gender-pay-gap.

Randstad USA. "Salary and Compensation Statistics on the Impact of COVID-19." Accessed June 7, 2021.

https://rlc.randstadusa.com/for-business/learning-center/future-workplace-trends/randstad-2020-compensation-insights.

Royal, James and Arielle O'Shea. "What Is the Average Stock Market Return?" *NerdWallet*, May 25, 2021. https://www.nerdwallet.com/article/investing/average-stock-market-return.

Soni, Sandeep. "Half of World's Female Entrepreneurs Are Denied Funding; a Third Faces Gender Bias from Investors." *Financial Express*, October 13, 2019. https://www.financialexpress.com/industry/sme/half-of-worlds-female-entrepreneurs-are-denied-funding-a-third-faces-gender-bias-from-investors/1734266.

Stengel, Geri. "Female-Founded Fintech Makes It Easy to Invest in Minority and Women Entrepreneurs." *Forbes*, February 3, 2021. https://www.forbes.com/sites/geristengel/2021/02/03/female-founded-fintech-makes-it-easy-to-invest-in-minority-and-women-entrepreneurs/?sh=2d1a160f48ea.

CHAPTER 10

Allianz Life Insurance Company of North America. "Despite Rising Influence, Women Report Steady Decline in Financial Confidence." June 24, 2019. https://www.allianzlife.com/about/newsroom/2019-press-releases/women-report-steady-decline-in-financial-confidence.

El Issa, Erin. "Women and Credit Through the Decades: The 1970s." *NerdWallet*, July 22, 2020. https://www.nerdwallet.com/article/credit-cards/women-credit-decades-70s.

Fidelity Investments. "Who's the Better Investor: Men or Women?" About Fidelity. May 18, 2017. Accessed June 7, 2021. https://www.fidelity.com/about-fidelity/individual-investing/better-investor-men-or-women.

Hunt, Vivian, Dennis Layton, and Sara Prince. "Why Diversity Matters." *McKinsey and Company*, January 1, 2015. https://www.mckinsey.com/business-functions/organization/our-insights/why-diversity-matters.

Mesch, Debra. "The Gender Gap in Charitable Giving." *The Wall Street Journal*, February 1, 2016. https://www.wsj.com/articles/the-gender-gap-in-charitable-giving-1454295689.

Moniuszko, Sara M, Maria Puente, and Veronica Bravo. "Ruth Bader Ginsburg Becomes First Woman to Lie in State: 8 Other Strides She Made for Women." *USA TODAY*, September 24, 2020. https://www.usatoday.com/in-depth/life/2020/09/24/ruth-bader-ginsburg-8-things-she-did-womens-rights/3502065001.

Norton, Leslie P. "Improving Women's Issues Leads to Better Investment Returns." *Barron's*, June 21, 2019. https://www.barrons.com/articles/nia-impact-capitals-go-any-where-portfolio-owns-companies-with-women-leaders-and-has-a-mandate-to-improve-the-world-51561159739.

Schlutz, Abby. "Future Returns: Investing with a Gender Lens." *Barron's*. May 21, 2019. https://www.barrons.com/articles/future-returns-investing-with-a-gender-lens-01558484404?mod=hp_PENTA.

Smith, Kelly Anne. "Here's Who Will Benefit the Most from the $59 Trillion 'Great Wealth Transfer'." *Bankrate*, September. 25, 2018. https://www.bankrate.com/personal-finance/great-wealth-transfer.

The Money Doula. "Homepage." Accessed June 7, 2021. https://www.moneydoula.org.

The Shed. "Homepage." Accessed June 7, 2021. https://www.womenmoney.org.

Totenburg, Nina. "Justice Ruth Bader Ginsburg, Champion of Gender Equality, Dies at 87." *NPR*, September 18, 2020. https://www.npr.org/2020/09/18/100306972/justice-ruth-bader-ginsburg-champion-of-gender-equality-dies-at-87.

Yoo, Tae. "Why Women Make the Best Tech Investments." *World Economic Forum*, January 20, 2014. https://www.weforum.org/agenda/2014/01/women-technology-world-economy.

CHAPTER 11

Cision. "New Study from Him for Her and Crunchbase Finds Uptick in Gender Diversity Among Boardrooms of VC-Backed Private Companies." March 1, 2021. https://www.prnewswire.com/news-releases/new-study-from-him-for-her-and-crunchbase-finds-uptick-in-gender-diversity-among-boardrooms-of-vc-backed-private-companies-301237018.html.

Credit Suisse. "Companies with Higher Female Participation at Board Level or in Top Management Exhibit Higher Returns,

Higher Valuations and Higher Payout Ratios, According to a Report by Credit Suisse Research Institute." September 23, 2014. https://www.credit-suisse.com/about-us-news/en/articles/media-releases/42376-201409.html.

Hello Sunshine. "Homepage." Accessed June 9, 2021. https://hello-sunshine.com.

Him for Her. "About Page." Accessed June 9, 2021. https://www.himforher.org/about-us.html.

Him for Her. "Homepage." Accessed June 9, 2021. https://www.himforher.org.

Hyder, Shama. "The Hidden Advantage of Women in Leadership - How Closing the Gender Gap Can Increase GDP." *Inc Magazine*, May 2, 2019. https://www.inc.com/shama-hyder/the-hidden-advantage-of-women-in-leadership.html.

Jakab, Spencer. "More Women on Boards, Fewer Dangerous Products." *The Wall Street Journal*, April 7, 2020. https://www.wsj.com/articles/more-women-on-boards-fewer-dangerous-products-11586284077.

Nasdaq. "Nasdaq to Advance Diversity through New Proposed Listing Requirements." Nasdaq press release, December 1, 2020. Nasdaq website. https://www.nasdaq.com/press-release/nasdaq-to-advance-diversity-through-new-proposed-listing-requirements-2020-12-01.

Shepherd, Ann and Gene Teare. "2020 Study of Gender Diversity on Private Company Boards." *Crunchbase*, March 1, 2021. https://

news.crunchbase.com/news/2020-diversity-study-on-private-company-boards.

Solomon, David. "Goldman Sachs' Commitment to Board Diversity." *Goldman Sachs*, February 4, 2020. https://www.goldmansachs.com/our-commitments/diversity-and-inclusion/launch-with-gs/pages/commitment-to-diversity.html.

The Coaching Fellowship. "About Page." Accessed June 9, 2021. https://tcfs.org.

Wamsley, Laurel. "California Becomes 1st State to Require Women on Corporate Boards." *NPR*, October 1, 2018. https://www.npr.org/2018/10/01/653318005/california-becomes-1st-state-to-require-women-on-corporate-boards.

CHAPTER 12

Abouzahr, Katie, Matt Krentz, John Harthorne, and Frances Brooks Taplett. "Why Women-Owned Startups Are a Better Bet." *Boston Consulting Group*, June 6, 2018. https://www.bcg.com/publications/2018/why-women-owned-startups-are-better-bet.

Astia. "Astia Launches $100M Fund." February 8, 2021. https://www.astia.org/news/Astia-Launches-%24100M--Fund.

Bennett, Jessica. "Do Women-Only Networking Groups Help or Hurt Female Entrepreneurs?" *Inc Magazine*, October 2017. https://www.inc.com/magazine/201710/jessica-bennett/women-coworking-spaces.html.

Bernard, Zoe. "The Next Women CEOs Who Could Take Their Companies Public." *The Information*, February 22, 2021. https://www.theinformation.com/articles/the-next-women-ceos-who-could-take-their-companies-public.

Bin Shmailan, Abdulwahab. "Compare the Characteristics of Male and Female Entrepreneurs as Explorative Study." *Journal of Entrepreneurship & Organization Management*, 2016. https://www.hilarispublisher.com/open-access/compare-the-characteristics-of-male-and-female-entrepreneurs-as-explorative-study-2169-026X-1000203.pdf.

Fessler, Leah. "Why Women-Run Startups Produce More Revenue." *Quartz at Work*, June 26, 2018. https://qz.com/work/1313962/why-women-run-startups-produce-more-revenue.

Kelly, Samantha. "31 Public Companies Founded by Women." *The Story Exchange*, February 10, 2021. https://thestoryexchange.org/31-public-companies-founded-women.

Kostka, Pam. "More Women Became VC Partners Than Ever Before in 2019 But 65% of Venture Firms Still Have Zero Female Partners." *All Raise* (blog), February 7, 2020. https://medium.com/allraise/more-women-became-vc-partners-than-ever-before-in-2019-39cc6cb86955.

Laporte, Nicole. "Bumble's Whitney Wolfe Herd on Making Nasdaq History and Breaking Barriers for Women CEOs." *Fast Company*, February 11, 2021. https://www.fastcompany.com/90603525/bumbles-whitney-wolfe-herd-on-making-nasdaq-history-and-breaking-barriers-for-women-ceos.

O' Connor, Clare. "When Bumble Goes Public Next Month, It'll Be with Whitney Wolfe Herd at the Helm, Who — At 31 — Will Be the Youngest Woman to Lead a Company through an IPO." *LinkedIn*. Accessed June 11, 2021. https://www.linkedin.com/posts/clare-oconnor_bumble-files-for-ipo-activity-6757375356933566464-pTxe.

Pearce, Kyle. "The Creative Mindset: 100+ Creativity Quotes from Entrepreneurs and Artists." *DIY Genius*, December 26, 2017. https://www.diygenius.com/the-creative-mindset.

SheEO. "Homepage." Accessed June 11, 2021. https://sheeo.world.

Shontell, Alyson. "Hundreds of Startups Go Public Every Year. Only 20 Are Founded and Led by Women." *Business Insider*, January 5, 2021. https://www.businessinsider.com/female-entrepreneurs-face-obstacles-taking-companies-public-2020-12.

Soni, Sandeep. "Half of World's Female Entrepreneurs Are Denied Funding; a Third Faces Gender Bias from Investors." *Financial Express*, October 13, 2019. https://www.financialexpress.com/industry/sme/half-of-worlds-female-entrepreneurs-are-denied-funding-a-third-faces-gender-bias-from-investors/1734266.

TheLi.st. "Homepage." Accessed June 11, 2021. https://www.theli.st.

The Muse. "Homepage." Accessed June 11, 2021. https://www.themuse.com.

Umoh, Ruth. "Black Women Were Among the Fastest-Growing Entrepreneurs—Then Covid Arrived." *Forbes*, October 26, 2020.

https://www.forbes.com/sites/ruthumoh/2020/10/26/black-women-were-among-the-fastest-growing-entrepreneurs-then-covid-arrived/?sh=18c8b5236e01.

West, Collin and Gopinath Sundaramurthy. "Startups with at Least 1 Female Founder Hire 2.5x More Women." *Kauffman Fellows*, October 17, 2019. https://www.kauffmanfellows.org/journal_posts/female_founders_hire_more_women.

INTRODUCTION TO PART II

Clear, James. *Atomic Habits: An Easy & Proven Way to Build Good Habits & Break Bad Ones.* New York: Avery, 2018.

CHAPTER 13

Carter, Christine. "What We Get When We Give." *Psychology Today*, February 19, 2010. https://www.psychologytoday.com/us/blog/raising-happiness/201002/what-we-get-when-we-give.

Chou, Tracy. "Where Are the numbers?" *Medium*, October 11, 2013. https://medium.com/@triketora/where-are-the-numbers-cb997a57252.

Kay, Katty and Claire Shipman. "The Confidence Gap." *The Atlantic*, February 19, 2010. https://www.theatlantic.com/magazine/archive/2014/05/the-confidence-gap/359815.

Knopp, Paul and Laura M. Newinski. "KPMG Study Finds 75% of Female Executives across Industries Have Experienced Imposter Syndrome in Their Careers." KMPG, October 7, 2021. https://info.kpmg.us/news-perspectives/people-culture/

kpmg-study-finds-most-female-executives-experience-im-poster-syndrome.html.

CHAPTER 14

Brizendine, Louann. *The Female Brain*. New York: Broadway Books, 2006.

Damour, Lisa. "Why Girls Beat Boys at School and Lose to Them at the Office." *The New York Times*, February 7, 2019. https://www.nytimes.com/2019/02/07/opinion/sunday/girls-school-confidence.html.

Ignatova, Maria. "New Report: Women Apply to Fewer Jobs Than Men, but Are More Likely to Get Hired." *LinkedIn Talent (Blog)*, March 5, 2019. https://www.linkedin.com/business/talent/blog/talent-acquisition/how-women-find-jobs-gender-report.

Jamali, Lily. "A Push to Get More Women on Corporate Boards Gains Momentum." *NPR*, March 5, 2020. https://www.npr.org/2020/03/05/811192459/a-push-to-get-more-women-on-corporate-boards-gains-momentum.

Kay, Katty and Claire Shipman. "The Confidence Gap." *The Atlantic*, February 19, 2010. https://www.theatlantic.com/magazine/archive/2014/05/the-confidence-gap/359815.

Mohr, Tara Sophia. "Why Women Don't Apply for Jobs Unless They're 100% Qualified." *Harvard Business Review*, August 25, 2014. https://hbr.org/2014/08/why-women-dont-apply-for-jobs-unless-theyre-100-qualified.

Schriock, Stephanie and Christina Reynolds. *Run to Win: Lessons in Leadership for Women Changing the World*. New York: Dutton, 2021.

CHAPTER 15

Andrews, Shawn. *The Power of Perception: Leadership, Emotional Intelligence, and the Gender Divide*. New York: Morgan James, 2017.

Bennett, Jessica. "Do Women-Only Networking Groups Help or Hurt Female Entrepreneurs?" *Inc Magazine*, October 2017. https://www.inc.com/magazine/201710/jessica-bennett/women-coworking-spaces.html.

Bennett, Jessica. "It's Not You, It's Science: How Perfectionism Holds Women Back." *TIME*, April 24, 2014. https://time.com/70558/its-not-you-its-science-how-perfectionism-holds-women-back.

Business Wire. "reacHIRE Launches the Aurora Platform for Companies Seeking to Engage and Retain Millennial and Gen Z Women." News. February 11, 2020. https://www.businesswire.com/news/home/20200211005309/en/reacHIRE-Launches-the-Aurora-Platform-for-Companies-Seeking-to-Engage-and-Retain-Millennial-and-Gen-Z-Women.

Carroll, Nina. "Madeleine Albright Talks about How She Became Secretary of State, Speaking up as a Woman and the Importance of Calling Out Wrongs." *USA Today*, August 26, 2020. https://www.usatoday.com/in-depth/life/women-of-the-century/2020/08/26/madeleine-albright-first-female-secre-tary-state-courage-fascism/5535871002.

Girl Scouts. "The National Stand Beside Her Movement." Accessed June 12, 2021. https://www.girlscoutshs.org/en/events/stand-behind-her-movement.html.

Kimsey-House, Karen and Henry Kimsey-House. *Co-Active Leadership, Second Edition: Five Ways to Lead*. Oakland: Berrett-Koehler Publishers, 2021.

Majeed, Monty. "If There Is Anyone Who Can Stand up for Women, It Is Women." Herstory. July 8, 2016. Accessed June 12, 2021. https://yourstory.com/2016/07/women-support-each-other/amp.

Parker, Kim. "Women in Majority-Male Workplaces Report Higher Rates of Gender Discrimination." *Pew Research Center,* March 7, 2018. https://www.pewresearch.org/fact-tank/2018/03/07/women-in-majority-male-workplaces-report-higher-rates-of-gen-der-discrimination.

Welsh McNulty, Anne. "Don't Underestimate the Power of Women Supporting Each Other at Work." *Harvard Business Review,* September 3, 2018. https://hbr.org/2018/09/dont-underestimate-the-power-of-women-supporting-each-other-at-work.

CHAPTER 16

Benton, Sarah A. "The Savior Complex - Why Good Intentions May Have Negative Outcomes." *Psychology Today,* February 6, 2017. https://www.scientificamerican.com/article/why-we-help.

Hello Sunshine. "About Page." Accessed June 12, 2021. https://hello-sunshine.com/our-story.

Kimsey-House, Karen. "Creating a Coaching Culture." *Co-Active Training Institute (Blog)*, May 29, 2019. https://coactive.com/blog/creating-a-coaching-culture.

My Confidence Matters. "Women: Confidence at Work." 2017. https://www.myconfidencematters.com/research-2017.

Nowak, Martin A. "Why We Help - Far from Being a Nagging Exception to the Rule of Evolution, Cooperation Has Been One of Its Primary Architects." *Scientific American*, November 1, 2012. https://www.scientificamerican.com/article/why-we-help.

The Muse. "About Page." Accessed June 12, 2021. https://www.themuse.com/about.

Walker, Kristi, Kristen Bialik, and Patrick van Kessel. "How Americans Describe What Society Values (and Doesn't) in Each Gender." *Pew Research*, July 24, 2018. https://www.pewresearch.org/social-trends/interactives/strong-men-caring-women.

CHAPTER 17

Ellevest Team. "Let's Disrupt Money ... by Talking about It." *Ellevest* (blog), May 14, 2018. https://www.ellevest.com/magazine/disrupt-money/talk-about-money.

Fidelity Investments. "Money Fit Women Study." 2015. https://www.fidelity.com/bin-public/060_www_fidelity_com/documents/women-fit-money-study.pdf.

Gandra, Akshita. "The Era of Women's Financial Independence." *Business Today,* August 22, 2018. https://journal. businesstoday.org/bt-online/2019/the-era-of-womens-financial-independence.

Krawcheck, Sallie. "Just Buy the F*ing Latte." *Ellevest* (blog), June 7, 2019. https://www.ellevest.com/magazine/personal-finance/just-buy-the-f-ing-latte.

Morrissey, Monique. "Women over 65 Are More Likely to Be Poor Than Men, Regardless of Race, Educational Background, and Marital Status." *Economic Policy Institute*, March 8, 2016. https://www.epi.org/publication/women-over-65-are-more-likely-to-in-poverty-than-men.

Taylor, T. Shawn. "For Steinem, Women Should Mean Business." *Chicago Tribune*, April 30, 2003. https://www.chicagotribune.com/news/ct-xpm-2003-04-30-0304300108-story.html.

Thomas, Jessica. "Sallie Krawcheck's Ellevest Reaches $1 Billion in Assets under Management." *Entrepreneur*, March 23, 2021. https://www.entrepreneur.com/article/367719.

CHAPTER 18

Burke, Elaine. "Diversity and the Data-Driven Workforce." *Silicon Republic*, November 10, 2017. https://www.siliconrepublic.com/advice/diversity-data-tracy-chou.

Eilperin, Juliet. "White House Women Want to Be in the Room Where It Happens." *The Washington Post*, September 13, 2016. https://www.washingtonpost.com/news/powerpost/

wp/2016/09/13/white-house-women-are-now-in-the-room-where-it-happens.

Grant, Adam. "Who Won't Shut up in Meetings? Men Say It's Women. It's Not." *The Washington Post*, February 18, 2021. https://www-washingtonpost-com.cdn.ampproject.org/c/s/ www.washingtonpost.com/outlook/2021/02/18/men-interrupt-women-tokyo-olympics.

McCurry, Justin. "Japan's Ruling Party Invites Women to Meetings – but Won't Let Them Speak." *The Guardian*, February 18, 2021. https://www-washingtonpost-com.cdn.ampproject.org/c/s/ www.washingtonpost.com/outlook/2021/02/18/men-interrupt-women-tokyo-olympics.

CHAPTER 19

Bennett, Jessica. "Where Women Made History … Right under Your Feet." *The New York Times*, August 13, 2019. https://www.nytimes.com/2019/08/13/us/where-women-made-history-right-under-your-feet.html.

Carducci, Poultney. "Seeing Is Believing: Female Role Models Inspire Girls to Rise." *World News Era*, October 9, 2020. https://worldnewsera.com/news/career-jobs/seeing-is-believing-female-role-models-inspire-girls-to-rise.

Gambino, Lauren. "'I Won't Be the Last': Kamala Harris, First Woman Elected US Vice-President, Accepts Place in History." *The Guardian*, November 8, 2020. https://www.theguardian.com/us-news/2020/nov/07/kamala-harris-victory-speech-first-woman-vice-president.

Warrell, Dr. Margie. "Seeing Is Believing: Female Role Models Inspire Girls to Think Bigger." *Forbes*, October 9, 2020. https://www.forbes.com/sites/margiewarrell/2020/10/09/seeing-is-believing-female-role-models-inspire-girls-to-rise/?sh=5f311d-fb7bf9.

CHAPTER 20

Bennett, Jessica. "It's Not You, It's Science: How Perfectionism Holds Women Back." *TIME Magazine*, April 22, 2014. https://time.com/70558/its-not-you-its-science-how-perfectionism-holds-women-back.

Campbell, Joseph and Phil Cousineau. *The Hero's Journey: Joseph Campbell on His Life and Work (The Collected Works of Joseph Campbell)*. Novato: New World Library, 2014.

Knopp, Paul and Laura M. Newinski. "KPMG Study Finds 75% of Female Executives across Industries Have Experienced Imposter Syndrome in Their Careers." *KMPG*, October 7, 2021. https://info.kpmg.us/news-perspectives/people-culture/kpmg-study-finds-most-female-executives-experience-imposter-syndrome.html.

Thibodeaux, Wanda. "3 Powerful Reasons to Compliment a Stranger Every Day (It's Not Just about Being Nice)." *Inc Magazine*, April 22, 2014. https://www.inc.com/wanda-thibodeaux/tk-powerful-reasons-to-compliment-a-stranger-every-day-its-not-just-about-being-nice.html.

CHAPTER 21

Chief.com. "Homepage." Accessed June 17, 2021. https://www.chief.com.

McKinsey & Company. "Women in the Workplace 2020." September 30, 2020. https://www.mckinsey.com/featured-insights/diversity-and-inclusion/women-in-the-workplace.

Zalis, Shelley. "How to Fix the Broken Rung." *Forbes*, December 10, 2019. https://www.forbes.com/sites/shelleyzalis/2019/12/10/how-to-fix-the-broken-rung.

CHAPTER 22

Brescoll, Victoria L. "Leading with Their Hearts? How Gender Stereotypes of Emotion Lead to Biased Evaluations of Female Leaders." *The Leadership Quarterly*, April 28, 2016. https://www.icos.umich.edu/sites/default/files/lecture-readinglists/Leading_with_their_Hearts-Brescoll%20%282016%29%20Leadership%20Quarterly.pdf.

Chief.com. "Homepage." Accessed June 18, 2021. https://www.chief.com.

Fottrell, Quentin. "'Women Are Judged for Being Emotional' — Yet It's More Acceptable for Men to Get Upset and Angry, Female Executives Say." *Market Watch*, November 29, 2019. https://www.marketwatch.com/story/serena-williams-got-angry-at-the-us-open-final-and-paid-a-heavy-priceworking-women-say-this-sounds-eerily-familiar-2018-09-10.

Helgesen, Sally. "Lean On." *LinkedIn*, November 24, 2020. https://www.linkedin.com/pulse/lean-sally-helgesen.

McKinsey & Company. "Women in the Workplace 2020." September 30, 2020. https://www.mckinsey.com/featured-insights/diversity-and-inclusion/women-in-the-workplace.

Psychology Today (blog). "Grateful Girlfriends Are the Best Stress Relievers." September 19, 2008. Accessed June 18, 2021. https://www.psychologytoday.com/us/blog/the-guest-room/200809/grateful-girlfriends-are-the-best-stress-relievers.

CHAPTER 23

Brown, Brené. *The Gifts of Imperfection: Let Go of Who You Think You're Supposed to Be and Embrace Who You Are.* Center City: Hazelden Publishing, 2010.

Burton M.D., Neel. "Our Hierarchy of Needs." *Psychology Today*, July 14, 2020. https://www.psychologytoday.com/us/blog/hide-and-seek/201205/our-hierarchy-needs.

Carter, Christine L. "What We Get When We Give." *Psychology Today*, February 19, 2010. https://www.psychologytoday.com/us/blog/raising-happiness/201002/what-we-get-when-we-give.

Cuddy, Amy J.C., Matthew Kohut, and John Neffinger. "Connect, Then Lead." *Harvard Business Review*, July–August 2013. https://hbr.org/2013/07/connect-then-lead.

Harris, Kamala. "Opinion: Kamala Harris: The Exodus of Women from the Workforce Is a National

Emergency." *The Washington Post*, February 12, 2021. https://www.washingtonpost.com/opinions/kamala-harris-women-workforce-pandemic/2021/02/12/b8cd1cb6-6d6f-11eb-9f80-3d7646ce1bc0_story.html.

Hookway, James. "Covid-19 Crisis Could Set Back a Generation of Women, U.N. Report Finds." *The Wall Street Journal*, November 26, 2020. https://www.wsj.com/articles/covid-19-crisis-could-set-back-a-generation-of-women-u-n-report-finds-11606414627.

TEDx Talk. "The Sophia Century: Lynne Twist at TEDxSandHill-RdWomen." January 5, 2013, Video, 17:46. https://www.youtube.com/watch?v=iz18RQ7UR3w.